D1164896

Enjoy!
Mary James

Mary James

dishes it out

Favorite Recipes and Personal Teaching Notes

Mary James dishes it out
Favorite Recipes and Personal Teaching Notes

Published by Roosters Gourmet Market and Gifts

This cookbook is a collection of favorite recipes, which are not necessarily original recipes.

Library of Congress Control Number: 2006909243
ISBN: 978-0-9789296-0-2

Edited by Mary James Lawrence

Designed and Manufactured by
Favorite Recipes® Press
An imprint of

FRP

P. O. Box 305142
Nashville, Tennessee 37230
800-358-0560

Art Director: Steve Newman
Book Design: Boulton Advertising + Promotions
www.boultonad.com
Project Editor: Cathy Ropp

Manufactured in China
First Printing: 2007
10,000 copies

To my children, Warner and Emily, who come to the table with a sense of adventure and a willingness to try anything.

INTRODUCTION

I have loved the process of writing this cookbook and reacquainting myself with recipes I have long forgotten. I started teaching cooking in the early '80s and have loved every minute of it. But getting started on this cookbook was difficult because I wanted to do something different. How could I share a part of me? Finally, I realized that I had to offer more than a recipe, and the idea of "teaching notes" was born.

My teaching notes are written as though I were standing in front of you teaching a class. They are the extra tidbits that might make a recipe easier, or give you an idea about the right equipment, or let you know why something works, or why it doesn't. They are the handwritten notes that I saw on students' recipes when they left class. My teaching notes are not absolutely essential, but hopefully helpful. They are the answers to questions that were frequently asked during class.

Another "issue" I faced was calling for brand names in the ingredient list. I feel that there are times when this is important and makes a difference in the recipe. When I finally realized that the "cookbook police" wouldn't come after me, I moved ahead. Where possible, I have offered alternatives, but if a brand name is listed it is preferred.

Equipment is another "issue." As with all activities, not just cooking, the job goes more easily if you have the right tools. (Ask any man who has a workshop.) So I have put together a list of tools that I think are the essential basics. Keep these on a magnet bar or in a utensil jar in your work area so they are handy. Hide them away in a drawer and you will forget you have them. In this book, I actually call for using these tools in the recipes.

You know the old saying "a picture speaks a thousand words"? Well, go to *www.maryjames.net* and you will find photographs of many of the recipes and their techniques. For example, it was hard to explain in words how to butterfly a beef or pork tenderloin. Go to the Web site and there is a video. Yes, I can be right there beside you showing you how. Getting ready for a party and want some ideas for your table? Go to the Web site for presentation and party ideas. You have a great idea you want to share or have had a party featuring recipes from *Mary James dishes it out*? Click on contact us, send a photo or idea, and it will be published on the Web site. And, finally, I know that I will continue to find recipes that I wish I had included in the book. They will be added to the Web site. It will be constantly evolving. Please visit often.

Not all recipes in this book are original to me. Some of the popular cooking school recipes were chosen for their teaching content. And many of the recipes from Roosters on the Run catering/deli operation were gathered from friends, family, and the community. I include them all here—Enjoy!

CONTENTS

KITCHEN ESSENTIALS

For years, I have preached in front of classes about the necessity of having the right equipment, from heavy-bottomed cookware to knives to tools. Good equipment makes you more efficient and makes life in the kitchen much easier and less time consuming.

HEATPROOF RUBBER SPATULAS—From the mixing bowl to the skillet, these spatulas can withstand any temperature. Perfect for scrambling eggs, stirring hot sauces, or scraping down a mixing bowl. Keep several sizes on hand. Wooden spoons are a thing of the past.

FLAT ROUX WHISK—Ideal for making sauces and gravies because it gets in the corners of the pan. Also perfect for pancakes, brownies, and stiff batters. It is also the perfect tool for folding ingredients.

BALLOON WHISK—Necessary when volume is needed or when you need to smooth a sauce or lumpy light batter.

VEAL/MEAT POUNDER—To flatten and smooth out chicken breasts, meat scallopinis, and butterflied roasts. Choose a pounder with a smooth pounding surface and offset handle.

OFFSET SPATULAS—Spread mayonnaise and peanut butter. Level batters in pans. Ice cakes. Because the handle is offset, you can spread evenly without your hand getting in the way. Works well as a turning tool, i.e., miniature crab cakes. Two sizes are needed, 4 1/2 inches and 8 inches.

LOOP CORER—Easily removes the core of apples and pears without waste. Seeds cucumbers and zucchini.

CITRUS REAMER—Wooden reamer for getting the most juice from lemons and limes.

MICROPLANES—# 1 tool to be introduced since I started cooking. Zests lemons, limes, and oranges. Grates nutmeg. Shreds cheeses. Two sizes are necessary, the fine cut and the ribbon cut.

SILPAT PAN LINER—Essential for cookies, rolls, and candies. Now there is no need for greasing and flouring pans. This reusable pan liner saves you time and keeps your pans like new.

COTTON KITCHEN TWINE—100% food-safe cotton twine for tying meats and poultry, a bouquet garni, or even a stack of magazines for the recycle bin.

PASTRY SCRAPER/DOUGH BLADE—This is the best cleanup tool in the kitchen. Use for gathering and transferring chopped vegetables. Use to lift dough and incorporate flour into dough at the beginning of the kneading process. Cleans work surface of flour and hardened bits of dough.

ICE CREAM SCOOPS—Not just for ice cream, scoops are essential for portioning everything from crab cakes to muffins. The size is printed on the blade, the bowl, or the handle. Frequently, food service scoops come with different colored handles which relate to their size. A #16 scoop holds 1/4 cup and has a blue handle—perfect for making jumbo cookies. Using a scoop creates uniform cookies, muffins, crab cakes, etc.

PASTRY WHEEL—The crinkled edge of this fluted pastry wheel makes any pastry look as though it's been cut using pinking shears. The rippled edge is appealing on lattice pastry strips, thin crackers, or pasta for lasagna or ravioli.

PASTRY BRUSH—For brushing on glazes and egg washes. You need two, one for sweet dishes and one for savory dishes.

PLASTIC SQUEEZE BOTTLES—Necessary for adding decorative touches to plates or mass producing an appetizer that has just a dot of sauce.

SPIDER—This wide, flat wire strainer is used to lift things from deep fat or boiling broth or water.

SILICONE BASTING BRUSH—Another new heatproof tool. This one is ideal for the BBQ—no more sizzled bristles.

GARLIC PRESS—Crushes garlic quickly and easily, eliminating the need for mincing.

INSTANT-READ THERMOMETER—Accurately measures the internal temperatures of meats, the doneness of a baked loaf of bread (190 degrees), or the temperature of water for dissolving yeast (105 degrees). Choose the model with a magnified 1-inch dial (60 to 220 degrees) for easy reading.

BISCUIT CUTTERS—Set of four with handles for easy cutting.

PASTRY BAG—Choose a large 14-inch bag for all-purpose kitchen duty.

PASTRY TIPS—Three all-purpose tips: #6 PT (plain tip), a #4, and #6 CS (closed star).

FRENCH ROLLING PIN—Tapered on the ends with no handles. This style pin facilitates even rolling.

SALAD SPINNER—Makes washing lettuces, greens, and herbs easy.

MESH STRAINER—A fine mesh strainer with a handle is perfect for washing berries, straining a sauce, or dusting powdered sugar over cakes and desserts. Two sizes are necessary, a small (5 inches) and a large (8 inches).

PERFECT BEAKER—My favorite liquid measuring cup. With six different measuring scales on the side of the cup, conversions are easy—tablespoons, cups, ounces, and milliliters.

FAT SEPARATOR—Quickly removes fat from meat juices—an essential tool when making Thanksgiving gravy.

GRADUATED MEASURING CUPS—A six-piece nested set for dry measurements ($1/4$ cup, $1/3$ cup, $1/2$ cup, $2/3$ cup, $3/4$ cup, 1 cup).

MANDOLINE—The mandoline slices, juliennes, and makes waffle cuts in several widths and thicknesses. Extremely sharp blades can make it dangerous to use. Novices should always use the guard.

TIMBALE MOLDS—Small, steep-sided cylinders that come in various sizes and are used to make flans, custards, cakes, and rice puddings. Custard cups can usually be substituted. Perfect for individual presentations.

Visit www.maryjames.net *for photos.*

Appetizers

▶ *Appetizers are meant to tease the appetite, not satisfy it.*

MARY JAMES

Appetizers
at a glance

Tenderloin of Beef

SERVES 24 TO 30 FOR COCKTAIL PARTY

A Rooster's cocktail buffet was not complete without Tenderloin of Beef on Focaccia (page 41).

Preheat oven to 450 degrees.

Trim tenderloin removing fat, silver skin, and chain. Fold tail piece under. Tie each piece at 2- or 3-inch intervals to create even pieces of meat. Lightly coat with Montreal steak seasoning.

Heat a heavy-bottomed ovenproof sauté pan over medium-high heat. Add enough oil to cover bottom of pan. Add meat and sear well on all sides. Resist the urge to constantly pick up and turn. It should take 3 to 4 minutes per side.

Transfer to preheated oven and cook for 15 to 20 minutes or until a thermometer reads 125 degrees. Remove from oven and allow to cool. Refrigerate for several hours before carving for sandwiches.
If serving immediately, remove from oven and let stand at least 15 minutes before carving.

MUSTARD SAUCE: Combine mustard and sour cream.

HORSERADISH SAUCE: Combine sour cream, mayonnaise, and horseradish.

For cocktail buffet, thinly slice tenderloin and present on large platter with bowls of Mustard Sauce and Horseradish Sauce. Mound split focaccia or rolls on the side.

1 (6- or 7-pound) beef tenderloin,
   untrimmed (4^1/2 to 5 pounds
   trimmed)
Montreal steak seasoning
oil

MUSTARD SAUCE
1 cup Dijon mustard
^{1}/2 cup sour cream

HORSERADISH SAUCE
^{1}/2 cup sour cream
^{1}/4 cup mayonnaise
3 tablespoons horseradish

TEACHING NOTES

- *If wings stick to sheet pan, just work under them with a metal spatula.*

- *Texas Pete is a medium hot sauce made in North Carolina and available in grocery stores. If not available, substitute your favorite wing sauce.*

- *If time does not allow you to make the blue cheese dipping sauce, purchase a blue cheese dressing and add 1 1/2 teaspoons soy sauce to each cup. Soy sauce wakes up a store-bought dressing.*

Hot Wings with Blue Cheese Dipping Sauce

MAKES 48 PIECES

Preheat standard oven to 425 degrees, convection oven to 400 degrees.

Cut off wing tips and discard. Cut through joint of remaining piece. Arrange wings in a roasting pan large enough to hold them in one layer.

Place in preheated oven for 45 minutes. Turn and bake another 45 minutes or until crisp. The fat will be rendered from the skin, leaving the chicken crisp and chewy.

Meanwhile, combine hot sauce and butter. Set aside. Remove wings from oven and while hot, toss in sauce. Serve with Blue Cheese Dipping Sauce.

BLUE CHEESE DIPPING SAUCE:
In food processor fitted with a steel blade, process garlic, mustard, and vinegar. With machine running, add vegetable oil. Add sour cream and 1 cup of the blue cheese. Pulse 1 or 2 times. Transfer to mixing bowl. Add remaining 1/2 cup blue cheese.

24 whole chicken wings

1/4 cup Texas Pete hot sauce
2 tablespoons butter, melted

BLUE CHEESE DIPPING SAUCE
1 large clove garlic
1 tablespoon Dijon mustard
2 tablespoons white wine vinegar
2/3 cup vegetable oil
2/3 cup sour cream
1 1/2 cups crumbled blue cheese

Grand Aïoli

MAKES 3 CUPS AÏOLI

APPETIZERS

With its beautiful color and dramatic presentation, many of Roosters' caterings included a Provençal Grand Aïoli platter.

AÏOLI: In food processor fitted with a steel blade, process garlic, and then add peeled potato, eggs, water, lemon juice, salt, and pepper. Process to combine.

Add the olive oil using the small feed tube which has a tiny hole in the bottom of it. This allows the oil to be added very slowly. Add a little more water if needed.

VEGETABLES: Steam vegetables (cauliflower, carrots, haricots vert, asparagus) to just done . . . tender-crisp. Refresh with cold water. Drain and store.

FISH: Steam salmon. Chill before serving.

AÏOLI
4 large cloves garlic
1 small new potato, steamed and warm
2 pasteurized eggs
2 tablespoons water
juice of 1 lemon
salt and pepper

2 1/2 cups extra-virgin olive oil

VEGETABLES
1 head cauliflower, cleaned and broken into bite-size pieces
baby carrots, rinsed
haricots vert, stems removed
asparagus, trimmed and tough stalks removed
cherry tomatoes
hard-boiled eggs, quartered

FISH (OPTIONAL)
salmon fillets

TEACHING NOTES

- *In France, the "aïoli monstre" is a festive occasion. Traditionally, it features boiled or steamed carrots, potatoes, and slender green beans, plus hard-cooked eggs, poached salt cod or salmon and crusty baguettes. And, of course, the guest of honor is a big bowl of aïoli, that thick, garlicky sauce of Provence. Choose your own favorite vegetables. Salt cod is most popular in France, but salmon is an easier alternative. Steamed shrimp are also excellent, but my favorite is escargot.*

- *This is a great dish for entertaining because it can all be done ahead and plattered just before guests arrive. Use for cocktail buffets with shrimp, or for dinners with a choice of seafood. Use the biggest platters available. Pay attention to color when arranging vegetables.*

- *Pasteurized eggs, available in the dairy section alongside all the other eggs, are specified in this recipe since the eggs are not cooked.*

13

TEACHING NOTES

- *Shrimp size is shown as the average number of shrimp per pound. In this case, 26 to 30 shrimp for a total of 52 to 60 in a 2-pound package. This is the smallest shrimp that should be used for this recipe. Use the largest shrimp you can find (and afford). Adjust cooking time as needed.*

- *Recipe works best in a convection oven but can be done in a regular oven. For a regular oven, heat salt for 30 minutes and cooking time will increase to 5 minutes or so.*

Shrimp Grilled on Salt with Pernod Dipping Sauce

Pat Opler, a great cook and teacher from Jackson Hole, Wyoming, first introduced me to the concept of cooking on salt. From her beautiful home overlooking the Snake River, anything would have tasted good, but it also tastes good back here in North Carolina.

Preheat convection oven to 500 degrees. Pat shrimp dry. Keep covered with paper towels to absorb any moisture.

Place salt on a sheet pan and transfer to preheated oven. Heat salt for 15 minutes. Remove from oven and quickly place shrimp on salt. Grind pepper over all. Return to the oven and cook for 3 minutes or until shrimp have turned pink. Remove from oven and using tongs transfer shrimp to serving dish, tapping off excess salt as you make the transfer. Serve with Pernod Sauce.

PERNOD DIPPING SAUCE: Combine mayonnaise, sour cream, lemon juice, shallot, and garlic. In the microwave, heat 1 tablespoon Pernod with saffron for 20 seconds. Combine with remaining saffron and add to mayonnaise mixture. Let sauce stand for 30 minutes before serving.

2 pounds raw shrimp
 (26- to 30- count), peeled, deveined
freshly ground black pepper

2 cups coarse sea salt

PERNOD DIPPING SAUCE
1/3 cup mayonnaise
2 tablespoons sour cream
2 teaspoons lemon juice
1 tablespoon minced shallot
1/2 teaspoon minced garlic

2 tablespoons Pernod
pinch of saffron

14

Mini Crab Cakes with Roasted Sweet Corn Basil Aïoli

MAKES 24 MINI CRAB CAKES

Combine bread crumbs, mayonnaise, egg, mustard, green onion, Worcestershire sauce, and Old Bay seasoning. Add crabmeat. Mix lightly. Do not overdo.

Place remaining bread crumbs in pie plate or pan. Set aside. Shape crab mixture into half dollar-size cakes. Coat with bread crumbs. Place on parchment paper-lined sheet pan and set aside.

Into a large deep skillet, pour vegetable oil to depth of 1/2 inch. Heat to 375 degrees. Carefully add the crab cakes and cook, turning once, until golden. Drain on paper towels. Serve topped with a dot of Roasted Sweet Corn Basil Aïoli.

ROASTED SWEET CORN BASIL AÏOLI: Preheat oven to 450 degrees. Place corn on baking sheet and roast until lightly charred.

Meanwhile, combine mayonnaise, basil, lemon zest, lemon juice, and garlic. Add cooled corn. Use as topping for crab cakes.

1/2 cup panko (Japanese bread crumbs)
1/4 cup mayonnaise
1 large egg, beaten
1 tablespoon Dijon mustard
1 green onion, minced
1 teaspoon Worcestershire sauce
1 teaspoon Old Bay seasoning

1 pound backfin or claw crabmeat, picked for cartilage

1 cup panko (Japanese bread crumbs)
vegetable oil for deep frying

ROASTED SWEET CORN BASIL AÏOLI
1 cup sweet corn
1/2 cup sour cream
1/4 cup mayonnaise
1/3 cup fresh basil, fine chiffonade
zest of 1 small lemon
1 tablespoon fresh lemon juice
1 1/2 teaspoons minced garlic

TEACHING NOTES

- *When shaping crab cakes, try to avoid having a thin knife edge that is so often seen on anything shaped into a patty. Instead, create a neat, straight, more squared-off edge. I do this by putting the crab cake on the counter and gently twirling with my finger tips then finish with a gentle double tap of the fingers on top of the crab cake.*

- *To chiffonade basil, stack the leaves, choosing the two largest leaves for the top and bottom of the stack. Roll up tightly like a cigar and slice into very thin slices. Once sliced, take the knife and make 3 or 4 cuts across the slices. Basil bruises and turns black if it is chopped.*

- *When cooking crab cakes, it is easier to turn them with a small offset spatula.*

15

Sushi Sandwich

MAKES 18 SANDWICHES

Pick up the cooked sushi rice from your local sushi bar and this becomes an easy impressive appetizer.

Place nori on counter. Top with a thin even layer of sushi rice. Top with single layer of salmon, more rice, then avocado, sprouts, and final layer of rice. Spread remaining nori sheet with a thin layer of prepared wasabi paste. Place paste side down onto layers. Put a sheet pan on top of the stack and press evenly to compact the sandwich. Cover tightly and refrigerate for 1 to 2 hours before serving.

TO SERVE: Remove from refrigerator and cut into 3 equal strips and then each strip into 3 equal squares. Cut each square on the diagonal to make triangles and serve.

2 (8-inch-square) nori sheets
1 1/2 cups cooked sushi rice
4 ounces sliced smoked salmon
1 avocado, thinly sliced
fresh sprouts
wasabi paste

Smoked Salmon with Wasabi Sauce

MAKES 48 (1 3/4-INCH) ROUNDS

WASABI SAUCE: Combine mayonnaise, wasabi paste, tamari, lemon juice, and ginger. Transfer to a squeeze bottle.

ASSEMBLY: Using a 1 3/4-inch-round cutter, cut pumpernickel into rounds. Squeeze a dot of sauce on the center of each round of bread, top with pieces of smoked salmon. Finish with a small dot of sauce and a cluster of alfalfa sprouts.

WASABI SAUCE
3/4 cup mayonnaise
1 tablespoon wasabi paste, or to taste
2 tablespoons tamari
1 teaspoon lemon juice
1 teaspoon grated fresh ginger

pumpernickel bread
8 ounces smoked salmon
alfalfa sprouts

Chicken Liver Pâté with Olives, Pine Nuts & Cognac

MAKES 1 1/2 TO 2 CUPS

This recipe was inspired by Hugh Carpenter, a favorite teacher at Roosters. He is a great chef full of verve, humor, and creativity. Thank you Hugh for inspiring us to think out of the box . . . and keep on writing those cookbooks!

Trim fat from livers and cut larger ones in half. In a 12-inch fry pan, melt butter and cook until it begins to brown. Add livers and garlic. Stir, cooking until livers lose their color and are cooked through. Do not overcook. Livers should just lose their color in the center . . . about 2 minutes.

Transfer livers and all pan juices to food processor fitted with a steel blade. Add thyme, lemon zest, salt, and pepper; purée. Add cream cheese. Process to incorporate. Add brandy. Process. Add pine nuts and olives. Pulse 2 or 3 times.

Transfer mixture to pâté mold or serving dish. If planning to unmold when serving, line dish with plastic wrap before filling. Mixture is very loose at this point. Refrigerate until firm.

TO SERVE: Unmold if desired or serve directly from crock or dish. Garnish with sprig of thyme.

1/2 pound chicken livers
2 tablespoons butter
1 tablespoon minced garlic

1 teaspoon fresh thyme
2 teaspoons lemon zest
1/2 teaspoon salt
1/2 teaspoon black pepper

4 ounces cream cheese, cut into small pieces
2 tablespoons Cognac or other brandy

1/4 cup pine nuts, toasted
1/3 cup oil-cured olives, pitted and chopped

fresh thyme sprig (garnish)

TEACHING NOTES

TEACHING NOTES

Parsley needs to be very dry to mince for gremolata. Classically, gremolata contains minced garlic also. It can be added here if desired. Gremolata is also a great garnish for vegetables. It is wonderful to toss with pasta and shrimp, too.

Gremolata Crab

SERVES 25 TO 30 FOR COCKTAIL BUFFET

An updated classic. An extremely quick-and-easy seafood appetizer for a cocktail party. Gremolata, a parsley lemon mixture usually meant for osso bucco, is key.

Pick through crabmeat for shell. Set aside. In mixer, combine cream cheese, mayonnaise, Worcestershire sauce, shallot, lemon zest, and lemon juice. Spread onto serving platter . . . about a 10-inch circle . . . creating a lip around the edge. Spoon chili sauce over the mixture. Mound with crabmeat. Just before serving, sprinkle heavily with Gremolata. Use a separate basket or tray for crackers.

GREMOLATA: Using a microplane, zest the lemon over the chopped parsley. Finally, on the cutting board add salt and continue to mince until well combined.

I pound fresh claw or
   lump crabmeat

I pound cream cheese
2 tablespoons mayonnaise
2 tablespoons Worcestershire sauce
3 tablespoons minced shallot
zest of I lemon
I tablespoons fresh lemon juice

1/2 cup Heinz chili sauce or your
   favorite specialty ketchup

crackers of choice

GREMOLATA
3/4 cup fresh parsley, finely chopped
zest of I lemon
1/2 teaspoon salt

Provençal Green Tapenade with Crostini

MAKES 4 CUPS

Every chef and housewife has their own variation on tapenade. Xavier's version has been a staple with our Provence tour groups and has now become popular here at home.

In food processor fitted with a steel blade, process garlic and parsley. Add almonds and process until a fine paste is formed. Add olives and lemon juice. Process until puréed. Add olive oil to loosen and to achieve desired spreading consistency. Season to taste with salt and pepper.

CROSTINI: Preheat oven to 350 degrees. Slice baguette into 1/4-inch rounds. Place on sheet pan. Brush lightly with olive oil. Bake until just beginning to change color. Remove from oven and, if desired, rub each slice with the cut side of a clove of garlic. Store in a tin.

5 cloves garlic
1/2 bunch parsley

1 cup slivered almonds

4 cups green picholine olives, pitted
juice of 1/2 lemon

olive oil
salt and freshly ground black pepper

CROSTINI
1 baguette
olive oil
clove of garlic (optional)

TEACHING NOTES

Picholine olives are milder and less salty than the typical pimento-stuffed Spanish olive. Picholines can be found in specialty food stores. Picholines with herbes de Provence work well in this recipe.

19

Lemon Ginger Tahini

MAKES 2 CUPS

In food processor fitted with a steel blade with machine running, drop ginger pieces and jalapeño through feed tube. Process until minced. Remove lid, add chickpeas, cream cheese, sour cream, sesame seeds, cumin, lemon zest and juice, salt, and pepper. Process to a purée. Add olive oil to achieve desired spreading consistency. Serve with crackers.

1-inch piece fresh ginger, peeled
   and sliced
1 jalapeño pepper, split and
   seeds removed

1 (15-ounce) can chickpeas, drained
   and rinsed
3 ounces cream cheese
1/3 cup sour cream
3 tablespoons sesame seeds, toasted
1 teaspoon ground cumin
zest of 1 lemon
juice of 1 lemon
1/2 teaspoon salt
freshly ground black pepper

olive oil
crackers of choice

Old-Fashioned Pimento Cheese

MAKES 1 QUART

Day in and day out, this was a Roosters on the Run best-seller. The extra-sharp Cheddar cheese is the key to this recipe.

Toss together Cheddar cheese and Parmesan cheese. Set aside.

In a separate bowl, combine pimentos, mayonnaise, Worcestershire sauce, pepper, hot sauce, and jalapeños. Add to cheese and stir to combine. Let stand for at least 2 hours before serving.

1 pound extra-sharp Cheddar
   cheese, grated
1/2 cup freshly grated
   Parmesan cheese

7 ounces diced pimentos
   (do not drain)
1 cup mayonnaise
2 teaspoons Worcestershire sauce
1 teaspoon black pepper
1 teaspoon Texas Pete hot sauce

jalapeño peppers, chopped (optional)

Curried Cheese Spread with Cashews & Cherries

SERVES 20 TO 30

Line a 6- or 7-inch tart tin with plastic wrap. Allow wrap to overhang the sides by several inches. Set aside.

Using food processor fitted with a steel blade, combine cream cheese, sour cream, and curry powder. Process briefly. Add cashews, green onions, and cherries and pulse to combine. Scrape down sides and pulse again. Remove from processor and spread into prepared pan. Pull wrap over top of mixture. Transfer to refrigerator.

TO SERVE: Unfold wrap. Invert mold or tart tin onto serving platter. Peel off plastic wrap. Top with chutney . . . spread to within 1/2 inch of edge. Surround with extra cashews and cherries (optional). Serve with rice crackers on the side.

11 ounces cream cheese
1/4 cup sour cream
2 teaspoons curry powder

1/2 cup cashews
1/2 cup green onions
1/2 cup dried tart cherries

Neera's pear cardamom chutney or chutney of choice

cashews (optional garnish)
cherries (optional garnish)
rice crackers or water crackers

TEACHING NOTES

This recipe can be done 3 or 4 days ahead. Unmold and top with chutney just before serving. Use a heart-shaped pan for a fun wedding shower or Valentine's Day presentation.

21

TEACHING NOTES

- *Trimming the Brie will be much easier if it is very cold. Often you see the puff pastry pulled to the top center of the Brie and twisted for a flower effect. This center piece of pastry frequently is not cooked completely and once the first piece is cut, the appearance is not good. Keep it simple with a smooth top and perhaps a pastry cutout or two.*

- *Other suggestions for topping the brie: Stonewall Kitchen's Roasted Garlic Onion Jam, Rothschild Farm Raspberry Salsa, Neera's Pear Cardamom Chutney, or any of your favorite sauces or chutneys . . . homemade or commercial.*

Brie in Puff Pastry

Quick, easy, and you can have a different flavor profile every time!

Line a sheet pan with parchment paper and set aside. Preheat oven to 400 degrees.

Trim rind from top of Brie only. Spoon raspberry chipotle sauce to within 1/2 inch of the edge. Place puff pastry sheet over Brie. Place a sheet pan on top of puff pastry and invert. Cut another piece of puff pastry and place over this side of the cheese. Wrap the bottom pastry up around the sides, pressing the edges of dough together to form a tightly sealed package. Using a sheet pan lined with reusable pan liner or parchment, invert wrapped cheese to its "final resting place." The pinched side (messy side) is now on the bottom.

Combine egg, salt, and water. Brush pastry with egg wash being careful not to drip onto the pan. Decorate top with extra pieces of pastry if desired.

Bake for 30 to 35 minutes or until golden brown. Let stand 10 to 15 minutes before serving. Transfer to serving platter. Sprinkle with fresh raspberries if desired. Serve crackers or sliced baguette on the side.

1 (8-ounce) round of Brie cheese
Fischer & Weiser raspberry
   chipotle sauce

puff pastry sheet, thawed
1 egg
pinch of salt
1 tablespoon water

fresh raspberries (optional garnish)

crackers or baguette

Chèvre Fondue

MAKES 2 CUPS

A fun appetizer for a small group of 6 to 8 people.

Place white wine and garlic in a small saucepan and reduce by half. Remove garlic. Add goat cheese, Comté cheese, and butter. Heat over low heat, stirring constantly until melted. Add mustard and brandy. Transfer to cheese fondue dish. Sprinkle with thyme and pepper.

Cut baguette into bite-size pieces and serve with fondue.

1/4 cup dry white wine
I clove garlic, pressed

II ounces goat cheese (chèvre)
4 ounces Comté cheese, grated
I tablespoon butter
2 teaspoons Dijon mustard
2 tablespoons brandy

1/4 teaspoon dried thyme
freshly ground white pepper

French baguette

Bacon & Tomato Dip with Black Pepper Potato Chips

MAKES 4 CUPS

This recipe always gets rave reviews and was used in the cooking school's corporate team-building classes to teach knife skills.

Combine the first 8 ingredients in mixing bowl. In food processor fitted with a steel blade, purée half and return to mixing bowl. Stir. Refrigerate for at least 2 hours before serving.

Serve with black pepper potato chips.

12 slices smoked bacon, diced, cooked, and drained
3 cups Roma tomatoes, peeled, seeded, and diced
1/2 cup mayonnaise
3/4 cup sour cream
I tablespoon Dijon mustard
1/4 cup diced green onions
1/4 cup fresh parsley, minced
1/8 teaspoon cayenne pepper

black pepper potato chips

TEACHING NOTES

Bacon & Tomato Dip with Black Pepper Potato Chips

- *When you want cooked bacon crumbles or pieces, dice cold raw bacon and then cook, stirring occasionally, until it is crisp. In cooking school, I always reminded students that bacon was meant to be cooked in an iron skillet. It seasons an iron skillet. Always keep Grandma's skillet close by for bacon, sausage, and burgers.*

- *Peel tomatoes by dipping into boiling water for 15 to 30 seconds. Remove. Run under cold water and skins slip off easily. To seed a Roma tomato, cut it in half lengthwise and squeeze. Tomatoes are now ready to chop.*

- *For 3 cups of diced tomatoes, buy 2 to 2 1/2 pounds Romas.*

- *This dip keeps well in the refrigerator for up to 2 weeks. After it has been stored, it will separate and will need to be stirred well.*

23

TEACHING NOTES

Vidalia Onion Cheddar Dip

It is important to grate the cheese yourself. Commercially grated cheese has anti-clumping agents added to keep it separated in the package. Also, you will be tempted to chop the onion in the food processor. Don't do it. The food processor is too strong and will break down the membrane of the onion causing unwanted acids to be released. Hand chop the onion . . . it makes a difference.

Feta & Roasted Pepper Dip

- *This makes a large amount but stores for several weeks in refrigerator. Use as a spread on sandwiches. I love it with grilled vegetables on focaccia or scallion bread!*

- *Buy feta cheese in a block. The crumbled feta tends to be overly salty.*

24

Vidalia Onion Cheddar Dip

MAKES 5 TO 6 CUPS

This much-requested recipe is actually one of the easiest in the book. The secret to its success is purchasing a truly sharp Cheddar cheese and grating it yourself.

Grate the cheese using a medium grating blade of food processor. Remove to mixing bowl and add diced onions. Stir to combine. Set aside. In a separate bowl, combine mayonnaise, Worcestershire sauce, hot sauce, and black pepper. Add to cheese and onion mixture and combine. Set aside for several hours before serving to allow flavors to meld.

1 pound extra-sharp Cheddar
  cheese, grated
2 cups diced sweet onion

1 cup mayonnaise
2 teaspoons Worcestershire sauce
1 tablespoon Texas Pete hot sauce
freshly ground black pepper

Feta & Roasted Pepper Dip

MAKES 5 CUPS

Colorful and oh so easy to prepare.

In food processor fitted with a steel blade with the motor running, add garlic. Add remaining ingredients and process until smooth. Transfer to storage container and chill. Serve with crackers or pita chips.

1 pound feta cheese
3 cloves garlic, peeled
1 (12-ounce) jar roasted red
  peppers, drained
1/4 to 1/2 teaspoon cayenne pepper
3 tablespoons olive oil

crackers or pita chips

Hot Spinach & Bacon Dip   MAKES 2 CUPS

Cook spinach according to package directions. Cool. Drain and squeeze until very dry.

Sauté bacon until crisp. Drain.

Stir together cream cheese, mayonnaise, green onions, parsley, Parmesan cheese, lemon juice, and cayenne pepper. Add bacon and spinach. Stir. Microwave on High power for 1 or 2 minutes or until hot, stopping microwave and stirring 2 or 3 times. Transfer to serving dish or chafing unit. Serve with crackers.

1 (10-ounce) package frozen
   chopped spinach, cooked
6 slices bacon, diced

8 ounces cream cheese,
   room temperature
1/2 cup mayonnaise
1/2 cup chopped green onions
2 tablespoons minced fresh parsley
1/3 cup Parmesan cheese
2 teaspoons lemon juice
1/4 teaspoon cayenne pepper
crackers of choice

Fresh Salsa & Guacamole   MAKES 5 CUPS

FRESH SALSA: For the best presentation, cut vegetables uniformly. In a medium bowl, combine all ingredients. Stir gently to combine. Add salt to taste. Refrigerate immediately.

GUACAMOLE: Halve avocado and remove pits. Scoop out pulp and mash. Add fresh salsa to taste.

TO SERVE: Place bowls of salsa and guacamole on platter and surround with chips.

FRESH SALSA
1/4 cup chopped Anaheim chiles
4 cups diced peeled tomatoes
1 cup chopped onion
3 tablespoons chopped fresh cilantro
2 teaspoons minced garlic
2 tablespoons lime juice
zest of half a lime
2 tablespooons vegetable oil
1/2 teaspoon salt
black pepper to taste

GUACAMOLE
4 large avocados
Fresh Salsa

TEACHING NOTES

Tortilla Crisps

When serving, arrange in shallow bowl or compote with tips of triangles reaching to the sky!

Want your crisps spicy? Add a sprinkle of cayenne. Want your crisps smoky? Use smoked paprika.

Won Ton Crisps

Won tons can be cut into any shape. For a decorative edge, use a crinkle pastry wheel. Use them plain or as a base for a spread or topping. Select different dried herbs for a different flavor profile. Or, butter miniature muffin tins and place buttered squares or rounds into tin and bake to create cups.

Tortilla Crisps　　MAKES 64 TRIANGLES

These tortilla triangles are good by themselves or with a spread.

Beat egg with salt and water. Brush onto each tortilla. Combine seeds, cumin, and paprika. Sprinkle heavily onto each tortilla. Using a pizza cutter, cut into 12 to 16 triangles. Arrange on baking sheet by alternating tips and tails of the triangles. Bake in preheated 350-degree oven for 15 to 20 minutes or until crisp. Cooking time can vary greatly depending on freshness of tortillas. Keep a close eye on them. Store in tins.

4 (10-inch) flour tortillas

1 egg
1 teaspoon salt
2 tablespoons cold water

1/4 cup flax seeds
1/4 cup sesame seeds
1/4 cup poppy seeds
1/2 teaspoon ground cumin
1/4 teaspoon paprika

Won Ton Crisps　　MAKES ABOUT 200 CRISPS

It's fun to play with the shapes and flavors of these crispy treats.

Preheat oven to 350 degrees. Combine dry ingredients of chosen flavor profile. Set aside.

Cut each won ton wrapper into 3 strips. On a buttered baking sheet, place strips close together, but not touching. Brush each either fat from chosen profile. Sprinkle with cheese mixture or herb mixture. Bake in preheated oven for 6 to 8 minutes or until golden and crisp. Remove and store in airtight tin.

1 (12-ounce) package square
　won ton wrappers

Choose a flavor profile:

FLAVOR PROFILE 1
3/4 cup butter, melted

1 cup Parmesan cheese, freshly grated
1 teaspoon herbes de Provence
red pepper flakes to taste

FLAVOR PROFILE 2
2 tablespoons toasted sesame oil
2 tablespooons vegetable oil

2 teaspoons curry
2 teaspoons dried tarragon
1 teaspoon powdered ginger
1/2 teaspoon salt

2 tablespoons toasted sesame seeds

Rosemary Popcorn

MAKES 16 CUPS

The concept for this recipe comes from an Atlanta restaurant. They weren't sharing the recipe for their bar snack, but it didn't take long to figure it out. And isn't stovetop popped corn so much better than microwave popcorn . . . do you remember?

1/3 cup grapeseed oil
1/2 cup popcorn

1 tablespoon finely minced
   fresh rosemary
3 or 4 tablespoons *Boyajian*
   rosemary oil
salt

Heat grapeseed oil in theater–style popcorn popper until the first whisp of smoke appears. Add popcorn. When it is half popped, quickly open lid and add minced rosemary. Transfer half of popped corn to serving bowl. Sprinkle with rosemary oil and salt. Add remaining popped corn and sprinkle with more rosemary oil and salt. Serve.

TEACHING NOTES

Rosemary Popcorn

Grapeseed oil is a good choice for popping corn because of its higher smoke point. Of course, vegetable oil can be substituted. The theater-style popcorn popper works extremely well for stovetop popping. It is a thin-bottomed pan (good heat conductivity) and has a stirring arm to facilitate even popping without burning.

Cheese Straws

MAKES ABOUT 250 (2-INCH) STRAWS

My hometown, Horse Cave, Kentucky, had a cheese creamery that produced extraordinary extra-sharp Cheddar cheese . . . rich and crumbly. This recipe was created for that cheese. It is no longer available, so substitute the sharpest cheese you can find.

1 pound extra-sharp Cheddar
   cheese, grated
1 1/3 cups butter, room temperature
2 teaspoons Tabasco sauce

4 scant cups flour
1 teaspoon paprika
1 1/2 teaspoons salt
1/2 teaspoon cayenne pepper, or
   to taste

Using electric mixer, combine cheese, butter, and Tabasco sauce. Combine dry ingredients and add to cheese mixture. Mix until well blended. Do not refrigerate. Transfer to cookie press fitted with the star pattern. Press out onto ungreased cookie sheet into 2- or 3-inch lengths. Bake in preheated 400-degree oven for 15 to 20 minutes or until golden brown. Cool completely before storing. Store in tins.

Cheese Straws

- *Press dough into long strips then cut into 2- or 3-inch lengths and transfer to baking sheet. I have had students tell me that they used a press from their child's play dough factory to make these cheese straws. Whatever works!*

- *Ovens vary greatly and, of course, if you are cooking in a convection oven, the cooking time will be less. However, flavor is better if cheese straws are cooked until they begin to have a light golden hue. Freezes well.*

27

TEACHING NOTES

- *Many of us hold on to our spices way too long. If they don't have a fresh pungent smell, then they are over the hill. Throw them away and buy new.*

- *Garam masala is an Indian blend of spices and is available in specialty food stores and ethnic markets.*

Indian Spiced Pecans

MAKES 2 POUNDS

This recipe is a mainstay in my Thanksgiving and holiday cooking and was my most requested recipe on WFMY's Good Morning Show.

Preheat oven to 350 degrees. Place pecans on baking sheet and toast in oven for about 10 minutes. Do not allow pecans to brown. They simply need to be warm to continue. Remove and leave oven on.

In a large skillet, melt butter. Add brown sugar, curry powder, ginger, garam masala, and salt. Stir to blend and heat until hot throughout. Do not cook this mixture. Add pecans to skillet and stir until well coated. Remove and place on baking sheet and place in oven with heat turned off. Leave oven at 350 degrees until this time. Allow pecans to dry. Remove from oven and transfer to baking sheet lined with paper towels. Salt to taste. Cool. Store in tins.

2 pounds pecan halves

3/4 cup butter
1/4 cup brown sugar
1 tablespoon curry powder
1 tablespoon powdered ginger
2 1/2 tablespoons garam masala
2 teaspoons kosher salt

Spicy Firecrackers

MAKES 36 TO 40 PIECES

This recipe was given to me by a friend, and made the rounds in the neighborhood. But when cookbook author Shirley Corriher visited Roosters and featured it in her syndicated column, we heard from people all over the country.

fat-free saltine crackers
Nantucket Off Shore Seasonings
    pueblo rub or your favorite
    herb blend or rub
red pepper flakes
I (10-ounce) package extra-sharp
    Cheddar cheese, grated

Preheat oven to 450 degrees. Cover the bottom of an 11×17-inch jelly roll pan with a single layer of crackers. Use a serrated knife to make final row of crackers fit. Sprinkle with rub, red pepper flakes, and top with an even layer of cheese. Place in a TURNED OFF oven and leave several hours or overnight. Break into pieces and serve. Don't try to have perfect squares.

TEACHING NOTES

Deviled Eggs

Add curry powder and top with chopped peanut garnish. Or add pieces of diced bacon and top with fresh minced parsley. But the ultimate . . . add truffle cream and top with black truffle pâté or caviar.

Deviled Eggs

MAKES 24 PIECES

Variations abound for deviled eggs. Create your own flavor profile.

I2 large eggs

¹/4 cup mayonnaise
3 or 4 tablespoons strong
    Dijon mustard
salt and freshly ground pepper
    to taste
paprika

Place eggs in saucepan and cover with cold water. Bring to a boil. Remove from heat and let stand for 30 minutes. Drain immediately and add scoops of ice (this facilitates peeling) and cold water. Peel eggs.

Slice eggs in half and remove yolks to a small bowl. Mash thoroughly with a fork. Add mayonnaise, mustard, and seasoning. Fill the egg whites with the egg yolk mixture (a pastry bag fitted with star tip makes it easier). Sprinkle with paprika.

Slow-Roasted Romas

MAKES ABOUT 100 PIECES

Good tidbit for hors d'oeuvre and cheese trays or use in salads and pastas.

Preheat oven to 300 degrees.

Remove stem end of tomatoes. Slice tomatoes into quarters. Scoop out seeds with your fingers. In a large mixing bowl, toss tomato pieces with olive oil and herbes de Provence. Place cut side up on sheet pan lined with parchment or reusable pan liner such as a Silpat.

Transfer to preheated oven and bake for three hours or until tomatoes are dry and chewy. Remove and store in refrigerator.

TO SERVE: Stand dried tomatoes on end in a small bowl. A great snack or a nice adjunct to a cheese tray.

3 pounds Roma tomatoes

3 tablespoons olive oil
1 tablespoon herbes de Provence

Twice-Roasted Garlic

MAKES 3/4 TO 1 CUP

This is a great little recipe to have in your repertoire. Use it for the Mediterranean Phyllo Pizza (page 131) or just smear it on a piece of warm, crusty French bread.

Leaving root end of garlic intact, cut off other end exposing tips of cloves. Arrange, cut side up, in a circle on microwave and ovenproof dish. Drizzle with olive oil. Cover with plastic wrap. Microwave on high for $1^1/2$ to 2 minutes. Garlic should be soft. Remove plastic wrap and bake in preheated 350-degree oven for 20 to 30 minutes or until edges begin to turn golden. Let stand until cool. Squeeze to remove cloves.

5 heads fresh garlic
2 tablespoons olive oil

Soups & Breads

▶

. . . soups and breads . . . comforting, satisfying and both can be prepared in advance . . . even more comforting and satisfying.

MARY JAMES

Soups & Breads

at a glance

Super Bowl Chili with a Southern Twist

SERVES 10 TO 12

Served over pinto beans and heaped with lots of toppings, this chili goes a step further.

In a heavy-bottomed Dutch oven or casserole, cover bottom of pan with vegetable oil. Add beef and cook until brown. Add onion and garlic and continue to cook until onion is translucent.

Add spices and stir to cook spices . . . about 3 minutes. Add tomato sauce, salt, water, and jalapeño. Stir to combine.

Bring to a boil and simmer, covered, over low heat for 1 hour . . . stir occasionally. Add more water if necessary.

PINTO BEANS: Wash dried beans and pick out any foreign material. Soak overnight or cover with water, bring to a boil and allow to cool before proceeding. Sauté 1 large chopped onion in vegetable oil. Add soaked or precooked beans. Add one ham hock for every 1 to 1 1/2 pounds of beans. Bring to a boil and simmer until tender . . . 1 to 2 hours.

TO SERVE: Place pinto beans in bottom of bowls and top with chili. Let guests choose their toppings.

3 pounds ground beef chuck,
(request coarse grind, if possible)
1 large onion, chopped
6 cloves garlic, minced

1 tablespoon paprika
6 tablespoons chili powder
1 tablespoon ground cumin
1 teaspoon dried oregano

1 (15-ounce) can tomato sauce
1 teaspoon salt
1 1/2 cups water
1 jalapeño pepper

PINTO BEANS
1 pound dried pinto beans

1 large chopped onion
vegetable oil
ham hock
green onions, chopped
sour cream
Cheddar cheese, grated

TEACHING NOTES

This Super Bowl menu was always a popular January class. Start planning the party now.

- *Vidalia Onion Cheddar Dip (page 24)*

- *Hot Wings with Blue Cheese Dipping Sauce (page 12)*

- *Super Bowl Chili with a Southern Twist (left)*

- *Jalapeño Cheddar Biscuits (page 47)*

- *Salad Greens with Fresh Fruit and Potato Sticks (page 55)*

- *White Chocolate Chunk Cookies (page 142)*

SOUPS · BREADS

Taco Beef Soup

- *For Vegetarian Taco Soup, use 1 to 1¹/2 cups TVP (texturized vegetable protein) in place of the ground beef. Sauté onion in a small amount of oil then add TVP and remaining ingredients and cook for 30 minutes. Add more water as needed.*

- *If you are a backpacker and have a dehydrator, this recipe works well for dehydrating. It also freezes well.*

Spain Meets Italy

Chorizo is a hard pork sausage from Spain. Spanish paprika is what gives this sausage its characteristic flavor. My favorite brand is Palacios Auténtico Chorizo de Espana. It is available in mild or hot.

Taco Beef Soup

MAKES 3 QUARTS SOUP

This recipe was always taught to scout groups. Easy to do and it worked well for their car camping trips.

In a 6- to 8-quart pot, cook ground beef with onion. Stir to break up the meat. Add tomatoes, pinto beans, tomato sauce, taco seasoning mix, and water (use the bean can to measure your water). Bring to a simmer (that means that it is barely boiling) for 15 to 20 minutes.

Top each serving with cheese and sour cream. Pass the chips.

1 pound ground beef
1 cup chopped onion
2 (14-¹/2-ounce) cans recipe-ready tomatoes
1 (27-ounce) can pinto beans (do not drain)
1 (15-ounce) can tomato sauce
1 envelope taco seasoning mix
27 ounces water

1 (12-ounce) package shredded Cheddar cheese
1 (8-ounce) carton sour cream
2 (10-ounce) bags tortilla chips

Spain Meets Italy

SERVES 6 TO 8

Spain's chorizo sausage and Italy's cheese tortellini combine into a luscious hearty soup!

Remove casing from chorizo. Split chorizo in half lengthwise then dice into ¹/4-inch pieces. Heat heavy casserole or stockpot. Add chorizo and cook just to render fat. Remove chorizo and drain fat from pan.

Add olive oil to cover bottom of pan. Add onion, garlic, zucchini, carrot, bell pepper, and tomatoes. Cook for 5 minutes or so. Return chorizo to pan and add stock, wine, paprika, basil, and oregano. Cook for 20 to 30 minutes. Just before serving, add tortellini and cook for about 5 minutes or until tender. Season to taste and serve.

1 (9.5-ounce) package Spanish chorizo sausage

olive oil
1 cup chopped onion
3 cloves garlic, chopped
2 cups coarsely chopped zucchini
1 large carrot, large dice
1 green bell pepper, small dice
1 pound tomatoes, chopped

5 cups beef stock
¹/2 cup red wine
1 teaspoon paprika
2 tablespoons dried basil
2 tablespoons dried oregano

10 to 12 ounces frozen cheese tortellini

Chicken Bouillabaisse

SERVES 12

SOUPS · BREADS

I was introduced to Pasta & Co., a Seattle take-out and specialty food store, at a culinary professionals meeting in the 1980s. This is an adaptation of their recipe. It has the flavors of the traditional seafood bouillabaisse from the South of France.

In a stockpot, heat enough olive oil to just cover the bottom of the pot. Add onions, leeks, and garlic. Sauté until tender. Add vermouth. Simmer for 5 to 10 minutes. Add tomatoes, tomato paste, parsley, Italian seasoning, fennel seeds, orange peel, saffron, water and chicken base. Simmer for 20 to 30 minutes.

Trim and rinse chicken thighs, cut into small bite-size pieces. Add to soup. Simmer just until chicken is tender . . . about 15 to 20 minutes. Remove orange peel. Add Pernod and red wine vinegar just before serving. Serve with Spicy Tomato Sauce if desired.

SPICY TOMATO SAUCE: In a sauté pan, heat olive oil and cook shallots until translucent. Add tomatoes, garlic, bay leaf, thyme, fennel seeds, bread crumbs, vinegar, salt, and cayenne. Cover, cook over low heat for 30 minutes, stirring frequently. Remove from heat. Remove bay leaf. Add orange zest.

Transfer to food processor. Purée. Add lemon juice, cream, and parsley. Process to combine.

olive oil
1 1/2 cups coarsely chopped onions
2 cups coarsely chopped leeks
2 teaspoons minced garlic

2 cups dry vermouth

2 (15-ounce) cans diced tomatoes, not drained
1 tablespoon tomato paste
1/4 cup chopped fresh parsley
3/4 teaspoon Italian seasoning
1 tablespoon fennel seeds
peel from 1/2 orange
1/4 teaspoon saffron threads
6 cups water
2 level tablespoons Minor's chicken base

2 pounds boneless skinless chicken thighs, trimmed

1 teaspoon Pernod or other anise liqueur (optional)
1 tablespoon red wine vinegar (optional)

SPICY TOMATO SAUCE
1/4 cup olive oil
1/3 cup minced shallots

4 large fresh tomatoes, peeled, seeded, chopped
5 cloves garlic, minced
1 bay leaf
1/4 teaspoon dried thyme
1/4 teaspoon fennel seeds
1/4 cup fresh bread crumbs
2 tablespoons white wine vinegar
1/2 teaspoon salt
1/2 teaspoon cayenne

zest of 1/2 orange

1 1/2 tablespoons lemon juice
1 tablespoon heavy cream
1 tablespoon minced fresh parsley

TEACHING NOTES

Chicken Bouillabaisse

- *To clean leeks, trim root end, split in half and run under cold water, separating layers to remove all sand and dirt.*

- *Substitute large shrimp for chicken to have a shrimp bouillabaisse. Be careful not to overcook the shrimp.*

- *If you don't have Minors chicken base, substitute 6 cups of your favorite chicken broth. Of course, this replaces the water, too. Taste for seasoning and salt as needed. Using Minor's base reduces the need for salt.*

Spicy Tomato Sauce

This recipe looks more difficult than it is. It is simply a matter of measuring ingredients and doing your mise en place (organizing your ingredients). It can all be done ahead.

35

TEACHING NOTES

This recipe is one of the best examples for the necessity of mise en place (organizing your ingredients) since there are several steps and techniques in the recipe i.e., making a roux, tempering eggs. Do your prep and be ready to go before cooking, then it becomes an easy, straightforward recipe

Wild Mushroom Soup

SERVES 6 TO 8

Harrison Turner taught this recipe every year in our popular Holiday Entertaining class.

MUSHROOMS: Add morels to 1 cup very hot water and let stand for 10 to 15 minutes to reconstitute. Strain through cheesecloth, reserving liquid. Slice thinly. Set aside for sautéeing. Trim stems from white mushrooms and shiitakes, reserving stems for soup base. Slice caps thin.

In a sauté pan, combine butter and olive oil until bubbly. Add all of the mushroom slices, including reconstituted morels, and sauté until juices have mostly evaporated. Add juice of 1 lemon. Set aside. While mushrooms are cooking, begin soup base.

SOUP BASE: In a 5-quart saucier or stockpot, melt butter until bubbly. Add leeks and cook until tender but not browned. Add flour and stir over medium heat for 2 minutes. Add chicken stock, whisking vigorously. Stir in mushroom stems and thyme sprigs. Simmer for 15 to 20 minutes. Strain, pressing juices from stems. Return soup to the pan.

TO FINISH: Whisk egg yolks and cream together to combine. Temper mixture by slowly adding 1 to 2 cups hot soup to egg and cream mixture while whisking constantly. Then add all the mixture to the remaining soup. Add strained morel liquid. Season to taste with salt and freshly ground black pepper. Heat gently just to finish cooking the eggs. Do not allow to boil.

Turn off heat and stir in butter. Transfer to shallow serving bowls and garnish with fluted mushrooms that have been sautéed in butter. Top with parsley.

MUSHROOMS
- 1 (1/2-ounce) package dried morels
- 1 cup very hot water

- 1/2 pound white mushrooms
- 1/2 pound shiitake mushrooms
- 2 tablespooons butter
- 1 tablespoon extra-virgin olive oil
- 1 lemon

SOUP BASE
- 3 tablespoons butter
- 1/2 cup chopped leeks
- 4 tablespoons flour
- 6 cups chicken stock
- stems of white mushrooms and shiitake mushrooms, chopped
- 2 sprigs of fresh thyme

- 2 egg yolks
- 3/4 cup heavy cream
- 2 tablespoons butter
- salt and freshly ground pepper to taste

GARNISH (OPTIONAL)
white mushrooms, fluted
parsley, chopped

Mediterranean Chickpea Soup

MAKES 3 1/2 QUARTS

Soak chickpeas overnight in cold water.

Drain and rinse chickpeas. In a 6-quart stockpot, combine chickpeas, pancetta, chicken stock, tomatoes, garlic, rosemary, and olive oil. Bring to a simmer and cook for 1 hour or until chickpeas are tender. Cool.

Purée cooled soup in blender. Season to taste with salt and freshly ground black pepper.

TO SERVE: Ladle hot soup into rimmed soup bowls. Drizzle each serving with a teaspoon of rosemary oil.

1 1/2 cups dry chickpeas

4 ounces pancetta or bacon, diced (see teaching notes)
12 cups chicken stock
3 medium tomatoes, peeled, seeded, and cut in chunks
2 cloves garlic, crushed
2 tablespoons fresh rosemary
1/4 cup olive oil
salt and freshly ground black pepper

rosemary oil (optional garnish)

TEACHING NOTES

Mediterrancean Chickpea Soup

- *Pancetta is frequently referred to as Italian bacon. However, there is one key difference in pancetta and American bacon. Pancetta is not smoked. So, if you need to substitute bacon for the pancetta, you should blanch it to remove as much smoky flavor as possible.*

- *To easily peel a tomato, cut an X on the bottom, not deep, submerge in boiling water for a few seconds. Remove. Run under cold water and skin will slip off easily. To seed, cut in half horizontally and squeeze gently. Use fingertips to remove as many seeds as possible . . . don't go crazy . . . a few are okay.*

- *Because of the tough skin of the chickpea, a traditional blender, not a food processor or immersion blender, is absolutely necessary for puréeing and achieving a creamy consistency to this soup.*

Roasted Pepper Fennel Soup with Pastis Cream

MAKES 5 TO 6 CUPS

In a large sauté pan, heat olive oil. Add fennel, carrots, shallots, and garlic. Sauté over medium heat until vegetables are tender . . . 10 to 15 minutes.

Add vegetable broth and undrained peppers. Bring to a simmer and cook for 20 to 25 minutes. Transfer to food processor fitted with steel blade. Purée. Season to taste with salt and freshly ground black pepper.

PASTIS CREAM: Whip cream to soft peaks. Whisk in lemon juice, zest, and pastis.

Serve hot or chilled, garnished with a dollop of Pastis Cream.

2 tablespoons olive oil
1 fennel bulb, coarsely chopped
2 carrots, sliced
2 large shallots, sliced
2 cloves garlic, chopped

4 cups vegetable or chicken broth
1 (12-ounce) jar roasted red peppers
salt and freshly ground black pepper

PASTIS CREAM
1/2 cup heavy cream
zest of 1/2 lemon

1 to 2 tablespoons pastis, Pernod, or sambuca

TEACHING NOTES

Roasted Butternut Squash Soup in Acorn Squash Bowls

SERVES 8

Preheat oven to 450 degrees. Cut squash in half and remove seeds. Slice into 1/2-inch slices and toss with just enough olive oil to coat. Place in single layer on sheet pan. Slice onion, smear with olive oil, and place on pan. Roast vegetables until tender and beginning to brown . . . about 30 minutes. Remove from oven. Cool.

Fit food processor with a steel blade. In batches, purée squash, onion and sage until smooth, adding some of the chicken broth to facilitate puréeing. Transfer to large saucepan. Add remaining broth. Whisk to combine. Bring to a simmer and cook for 10 to 15 minutes. Serve topped with a small dollop of sour cream and a fresh sage leaf.

SQUASH BOWLS: Preheat oven to 450 degrees. Slice off top third of squash. Scoop out seeds and stringy membranes. Cut a very thin slice off bottom of each squash to create a stable base. Rub inside and outside with olive oil. Place upright on baking sheet and bake for about 30 to 45 minutes or until squash is tender and top edges are golden.

3 pounds butternut squash, peeled
1 medium onion
olive oil

5 cups chicken broth
1 tablespoon fresh sage

sour cream (garnish)
fresh sage leaves (garnish)

SQUASH BOWLS
acorn squash (one per serving)
olive oil

Tomato Basil Soup

MAKES 4 QUARTS

Years ago, I took a group to the Orchard Inn in Saluda, North Carolina, for a few days of cooking classes and R&R. This recipe, with a few adaptations, was a favorite of the group.

In a large stockpot, heat olive oil and sauté onion until tender. Add flour, stirring to quickly cook the flour. Whisk in milk and chicken stock all at once. Continue to cook and stir until thickened. Add tomato pieces, tomato juice, parsley, basil (yes, 1/4 cup dried basil is correct), and salt. Bring to a simmer and cook for 15 to 20 minutes. Season with freshly ground black pepper.

Ladle hot soup into bowls. Using a cheese plane, shave curls of Parmesan cheese over soup and serve.

1/2 cup olive oil
I large onion, chopped
1/2 cup flour

2 cups milk
I (14-ounce) can chicken broth

I (28-ounce) can tomato
    petite pieces
I (46-ounce) can tomato juice
1/2 cup fresh parsley
1/4 cup dried basil
I 1/2 to 2 teaspoons salt
freshly ground black pepper

Parmesan cheese

Vichyssoise

MAKES 2 QUARTS

Combine potatoes, onions, chicken stock, water, and salt in large saucepan. Cook until tender. Using the immersion blender, carefully purée mixture. Stir in cream, oversalt slightly. Chill overnight. Garnish with fresh chives.

5 cups diced peeled potatoes
4 cups thinly sliced yellow onions
2 cups chicken stock
2 cups water
2 teaspoons salt

I cup heavy cream

1/2 cup chives

TEACHING NOTES

Tomato Basil Soup

- *This soup is very quick to make. Go ahead and make the full recipe. It freezes. The label on canned tomatoes seems to change frequently. Just choose the one that is pieces or get out your knife and start chopping!*

- *Domaine Chandon, the California winery, popularized a cream of tomato soup with a puff pastry crown. This soup works well for this presentation. Cut rounds of puff pastry slightly larger than diameter of individual ovenproof serving bowls. Fill each bowl 3/4 full. Brush edge of bowl with egg wash and press rounds onto top of bowls. Brush pastry with egg wash being careful not to let it run onto the bowls. Bake in preheated 375-degree oven until puffed and golden. Serve immediately.*

TEACHING NOTES

Chilled Kiwi Cucumber Soup

MAKES I QUART

Make this soup extra special by adding a scoop of sorbet just before serving.

Purée cucumber and kiwi in blender or food processor. With machine running, add olive oil, sugar and a pinch of salt. Chill. To serve, add a small scoop of your favorite sorbet.

I large cucumber, peeled, halved, and seeded
5 firm but ripe kiwi, peeled
⅓ cup olive oil
I teaspoon sugar
pinch of salt

sorbet (your choice: strawberry or basil or passion fruit, etc.)

Strawberry Soup with Chocolate Curls

MAKES SIX (6-OUNCE) SERVINGS

Stem strawberries and cut into halves or quarters. Combine with wine, grendadine, and cinnamon stick in a medium saucepan. Bring to a boil. Reduce heat and simmer for 10 minutes. Remove cinnamon stick. Purée using an immersion blender, blender, or food processor. Chill. Serve topped with chocolate curls.

2 (16-ounce) cartons fresh strawberries

I cup red wine
I cup grenadine syrup
I cinnamon stick

Focaccia

MAKES 48 SQUARES FOR COCKTAIL SANDWICHES

Use this recipe for everything from cocktail buffets to lunchtime sandwiches. It was always the first recipe I handed to interns and new employees.

Combine flour, yeast, and salt. Stir with a rubber spatula to combine. Combine water and oil into one container. Make a well in center of flour and add water and oil all at once. Stir well to combine into a mass of dough. Turn out onto floured counter and knead. Add more flour as necessary to achieve a smooth dough that springs back to the touch. Dough should be soft but not sticky. Place in bowl and coat with small amount of oil. Cover and let rise until doubled in bulk . . . about 1 hour.

Drizzle 2 tablespoons or so of olive oil on 11×17-inch sheet pan. Flip dough from bowl directly onto pan. Press dough evenly to corners. Let rise in warm place for 45 minutes to 1 hour. Make depressions in dough using fingertips. Drizzle with rosemary oil or olive oil and sprinkle with sea salt and rosemary. Bake in preheated 400-degree oven for 20 to 25 minutes or until golden. (Convection ovens will take less time and is the preferred method.)

5¹/4 cups bread flour

5 1/4 cups bread flour
2 tablespoons yeast
1 tablespoon salt
2 1/4 cups warm water
1/2 cup olive oil

rosemary oil or olive oil
Maldon sea salt
fresh rosemary

TEACHING NOTES

- *Variations abound. Tuck garlic slivers and/or sprigs of rosemary into dough after placing in pan, before final rise. Change all or part of the olive oil to a flavored oil i.e., rosemary, garlic, or basil oil.*

- *For a great sandwich, cut bread into sandwich-size squares and fill with grilled eggplant, goat cheese, fresh tomato slice, and arugula . . . don't forget the freshly ground black pepper.*

- *Excluding rising time, this recipe takes less time that it would take you to go to the grocery store and buy a loaf of bread.*

41

TEACHING NOTES

- *Whenever a recipe calls for diced, cooked bacon, always dice the bacon when it is very cold and raw. Place in iron skillet and cook over low heat stirring occasionally. Perfect, uniform product for salad, garnishes, etc.*

- *Olive oil can be substituted for the walnut oil. Of course, you just won't have as rich a walnut flavor. Or use rosemary, basil, or garlic oils.*

Olive & Walnut Fougasse

MAKES 2 FLAT BREADS

There are as many varieties of fougasse as there are chefs in the south of France. This is just one of my favorites.

In a glass measuring cup, combine milk and water and microwave on high for about 30 seconds or to a temperature of 110 degrees . . . very warm, not hot. Add walnut oil.

In bowl of a food processor fitted with a steel blade, combine flours, yeast, sugar, and salt. Pulse to combine. With the machine running, add warm milk and water mixture. Process until dough forms a ball. Continue processing for 60 seconds. Add bacon, olives, and walnuts. Process just to incorporate.

Remove dough from food processor. Knead a couple of times and place in oiled bowl, rotating dough to coat with oil. Cover and let rise until doubled in bulk.

Punch dough down and divide into 2 portions. Press into a free-form oval/ rectangle. Place on a baking sheet. Now visualize the veins of a leaf . . . lines going to an imaginary center vein. With a sharp knife, slash three lines (veins) through each side of the dough without cutting all the way to the outside edge . . . just through to the pan's surface. Pull openings slightly apart. Brush with walnut oil. Let rise until doubled in bulk. Bake in preheated 375-degree oven for 15 to 20 minutes or until golden. Cool on rack.

1/2 cup milk

1/2 cup water

1/4 cup walnut oil, room temperature

2 cups bread flour

1/2 cup whole wheat flour

1 tablespoon fast-rising yeast

2 teaspoons sugar

1 teaspoon dried rosemary

1/2 teaspoon dried savory

1/2 teaspoon dried thyme

1/4 teaspoon salt

1/2 pound bacon, diced and cooked crisp

1/4 cup oil-cured black olives, chopped

1 cup walnuts, chopped

www.maryjames.net

Olive Bread

This bread is perfect for cheese trays, sandwiches, and panini.

In a measuring cup, combine water and olive oil. Set aside

In food processor fitted with a steel blade, process flours, salt, and yeast just to combine. With the machine running, pour water and olive oil mixture through feed tube. Process until dough forms a ball. Add the olives and process just until they are coarsely chopped and incorporated in the dough. Remove dough from processor to a floured surface. Knead a few times to achieve a soft, smooth dough. Drizzle olive oil into a bowl and roll dough to coat. Set aside and let rise until doubled in bulk . . . about 1 hour.

Remove dough from bowl and divide in half. Shape into round loaves or baguette shape or divide into 3 pieces and braid. Place on a baking sheet that has been dusted with cornmeal. Let rise until doubled in bulk, about 45 minutes.

Bake in a preheated 400-degree oven for about 25 to 30 minutes.

1 1/4 cups water
1/4 cup olive oil

2 3/4 cups bread flour
1/2 cup whole wheat flour
1 teaspoon salt
1 1/2 teaspoons instant
    fast-rising yeast

3/4 cup kalamata or oil-cured black olives

cornmeal

TEACHING NOTES

Not sure your loaf of bread is done? Forget the thump test! Use your instant-read thermometer. The internal temperature of softer breads and quick breads should be 190 degrees when done, and harder, crustier breads should be 200 to 210 degrees.

43

Scallion Bread

MAKES 48 (2-INCH) SQUARES

Perfect as a sandwich bread or alongside a bowl of soup.

Combine yeast, flour, and salt. Combine water and olive oil. Add to flour mixture. Stir to mix well. Turn out onto a floured counter and knead until smooth and elastic, adding small amounts of more flour to keep dough from being sticky. Drizzle a small amount of oil in mixing bowl, add dough and rotate to coat with oil. Set aside and let rise until doubled in bulk . . . about 1 hour. Preheat oven to 400 degrees.

Brush an 11×17-inch jelly roll pan with olive oil. Flip dough from bowl directly onto pan. Press dough evenly to corners. Make dimples into dough by pressing with fingertips. Sprinkle with cheese of choice or a combination of cheeses. Combine olive oil and green onions. Scatter over top. Sprinkle with kosher salt. Let rise for 30 to 40 minutes. Bake in preheated 400-degree oven for 20 to 25 minutes.

2 teaspoons fast-rising yeast
6 cups flour
2 teaspoons kosher salt

2 1/2 cups hot water
1/4 cup olive oil

1/2 cup Parmesan or romano or asiago cheese, grated

2 tablespoons olive oil
1/2 cup chopped green onion tops

kosher salt

Easter Bread

MAKES 1 (10- TO 12-INCH) RING

Fun and festive for the Spring holiday season. It has always been a family favorite.

In a large bowl, mix 1 cup flour, sugar, salt, and yeast. Set aside.

In a saucepan, combine milk and 2 tablespoons butter. Heat over low heat until liquid is warm (butter does not have to melt). Gradually add this mixture to dry ingredients and beat for 2 minutes at medium speed of electric mixer . . . scraping down bowl. Add eggs and 1/2 cup flour, or enough flour to make a thick batter. Beat at high speed for 2 minutes, scraping bowl occasionally. Stir in enough additional flour to make a soft dough. Turn out onto lightly floured board; knead until smooth and elastic, about 8 to 10 minutes. Place in greased bowl; turn to grease top. Cover; let rise in warm place until doubled in bulk . . . about 1 hour.

Combine apricots, almonds, and fennel seeds. Punch dough down; turn out onto lightly floured board. Knead in fruit mixture. Divide dough in half. Roll each half into a 24-inch rope. Twist ropes together loosely and form into ring on baking sheet lined with parchment or a reuseable pan liner. Brush with melted butter. Tuck uncooked dyed eggs into spaces in the twist. Cover; let rise in warm place until doubled in bulk . . . about 1 hour.

Bake at 350 degrees for about 30 to 35 minutes or until done. Remove from baking sheet and cool on wire rack. Drizzle icing over bread and decorate with sprinkles.

ICING: Combine 1 cup of confectioners' sugar with enough melted butter to achieve drizzling consistency.

2¹/4 to 3¹/4 cup flour, divided
¹/4 cup sugar
1 teaspoon salt
1 package dry yeast

²/3 cup milk
2 tablespoons butter

2 eggs, room temperature
¹/2 cup dried apricots
¹/4 cup slivered almonds
¹/2 teaspoon fennel seeds
2 tablespoons melted butter

5 uncooked eggs, dyed

ICING
powdered sugar
melted butter

pastel sprinkles

TEACHING NOTES

Don't be afraid of yeast! Because this recipe includes eggs in the dough, it is the perfect bread for the beginning baker and was always in our basics bread class. Don't hesitate to substitute other dried fruits such as cherries or cranberries for the apricots. The dyed eggs cook as the bread bakes making for a complete breakfast.

45

TEACHING NOTES

- *Mixing ingredients quickly and not overmixing is crucial to achieving a tender biscuit. The dough will be very sticky when first mixed and is best left overnight in the refrigerator before rolling out and cutting into biscuits.*

- *I have specified good ole southern White Lily flour. It is of exceptional quality and is made from soft winter wheat. It yields a superb biscuit. If it is not available to you, then choose any all-purpose flour.*

Angel Biscuits

MAKES 12 DOZEN

I have made thousands of these biscuits. It is the recipe of choice for the petite country ham biscuits that were so popular at Roosters on the Run.

Combine flour, baking powder, baking soda, salt, sugar, and yeast. Stir to combine well. Cut in shortening. Add buttermilk all at once, mixing quickly with a spoon. Do not overmix. Transfer to a clean bowl. Cover with a piece of plastic wrap placed on the surface of the dough to completely seal. Refrigerate overnight. For immediate use, let stand at room temperature for a minimum of 1 to 2 hours before proceeding . . . overnight is definitely best.

TO USE: Turn 1/3 of the dough onto floured surface. It is sticky but do not add more flour. Just sprinkle top and pat into flat circle. Roll dough to 1/4-or 1/2-inch thickness. Cut with biscuit cutter and place on baking sheet lined with parchment or reusable pan liner. Let rise in warm place . . . about 45 minutes. Bake in preheated 400-degree oven for 10 to 12 minutes or until golden brown.

5 cups White Lily all-purpose flour
1 tablespoon baking powder
1 teaspoon baking soda
1 tablespoon salt
3 tablespoons sugar
1 tablespoon instant yeast
3/4 cup shortening

2 1/2 cups buttermilk

46

Jalapeño Cheddar Biscuits

MAKES 48 (2-INCH) BISCUITS

Preheat oven to 425 degrees. In a medium bowl, combine flour, baking powder, baking soda, and salt. Cut in butter until mixture resembles coarse meal. Stir in cheese and jalapeños. Add sour cream and combine into a soft, but not sticky, dough. On a floured surface, pat out into a 1/2-inch thickness. Cut with biscuit cutter. Bake on ungreased baking sheet. Bake in preheated oven for 15 minutes or until golden.

3 cups all-purpose flour

1 tablespoon plus 1 teaspoon baking powder

1 teaspoon baking soda

1 teaspoon salt

1/2 cup butter, cut up

3 cups sharp Cheddar cheese, grated

6 pickled jalapeños, seeded and diced

2 cups sour cream

TEACHING NOTES

Never overwork biscuit dough, or it will be tough. Stir quickly to combine. These freeze very well.

For softer biscuits, place on baking sheet with biscuits touching each other.

TEACHING NOTES

Don't overmix muffin batter or muffins will be tough.

Raspberry Muffins

MAKES 12 MUFFINS

I got this recipe from a California bed and breakfast, the name of which escapes me now. It is my favorite homemade muffin . . . light and yummy!

Preheat oven to 350 degrees.

Combine flours, sugars, cinnamon, and baking powder. Melt butter. Cool slightly. Add milk and egg to butter. Add milk mixture to flour mixture. Stir to just combine. Add lemon zest and raspberries. Stir lightly. Spoon into paper-lined muffin tins. Fill cups 2/3 full.

TOPPING: Combine topping ingredients. Spoon heavily onto batter. Bake for 20 to 25 minutes or until tops spring back when touched.

3/4 cup flour
3/4 cup whole wheat flour
1/2 cup sugar
1/4 cup brown sugar
2 teaspoons cinnamon
2 teaspoons baking powder

1/2 cup butter
1/2 cup milk
1 egg
zest of 1 lemon
1/2 pint fresh raspberries

TOPPING
1/2 cup light brown sugar
1/4 cup flour
1/2 cup pecans, chopped
1/4 cup oatmeal
3 tablespoons butter, melted

Salads & Dressings ▶

. . . finding balance between oil and vinegar is an art.

MARY JAMES

Salads & Dressings

at a glance

Cranberry Almond Chicken Salad

MAKES 2¹/₂ QUARTS

When Roosters on the Run closed, there were many customers who were crying the blues over no more Cranberry Almond Chicken Salad.

Rub each chicken breast with olive oil and 1 teaspoon balsamic chicken rub. Prepare charcoal grill or preheat gas grill. Grill chicken until done. Cooking time varies with size of breasts. Cool. Dice into ¹/2- to ³/4-inch cubes.

Add mayonnaise, balsamic chicken rub, cranberries, and almonds to chicken. Stir to combine.

- 3 pounds boneless skinless chicken breasts
- 2 tablespoons Colorado Spice balsamic chicken rub
- 2 tablespoons olive oil

- 1¹/3 cups mayonnaise
- 2¹/2 tablespoons Colorado Spice balsamic chicken rub
- 1 cup dried cranberries
- 1¹/4 cups slivered almonds, toasted

SALADS · DRESSINGS

TEACHING NOTES

Sage-Scented Chicken Salad

Bone-in chicken breasts will always give you more flavor and it is basically just a one-step process to pull the skin and meat from the bone. For the ultimate flavor, refrigerate this chicken salad for at least a few hours before serving.

Sage-Scented Chicken Salad

MAKES 2 QUARTS

From Roosters on the Run, this was our very popular basic chicken salad.

In a large saucepan or stockpot, cover chicken with water. Add carrot, celery, and onion. Bring to a boil, reduce heat, Cover and simmer for 10 minutes. Turn off heat and let stand for 1 hour. Lift chicken from broth. When cool enough to handle, remove skin and pull whole breast from bone. Tear meat into bite-size pieces.

In a medium mixing bowl, combine mayonnaise, sour cream, sage, salt, and pepper. Add chicken and celery. Stir to combine.

- 5 pounds bone-in chicken breasts (6 to 7 cups pulled chicken)
- 1 carrot, cut in pieces
- 1 stalk celery, cut in 4 pieces
- ¹/2 onion, cut in 3 pieces

- 3/4 cup mayonnaise
- 3/4 cup sour cream
- 2 tablespoons dried sage
- 2 teaspoons salt
- freshly ground black pepper

- 1¹/2 cups diced celery

SALADS · DRESSINGS

TEACHING NOTES

- *MJ's 3 rules for cooking chicken for salads . . . Use bone-in breasts, don't overcook, and always pull the meat. Follow these 3 rules and you will always have a tender, succulent end result.*

- *Pappadums are available at ethnic markets. They are an excellent accompaniment to salad and soups, and are also popular as a low-fat snack.*

Lemon Ginger Chicken Salad

Wash chicken thoroughly and place in stockpot with ginger, celery tops, onion, and bay leaves. Cover with cold water. Bring to a boil and simmer for 15 minutes. Turn off heat, cover, and let stand for 1 hour. Remove chicken breasts. Remove skin and pull meat from bones. Tear into bite-size pieces and set aside.

Combine mayonnaise, sour cream, grated ginger, sugar, lemon zest, ground ginger, and salt. Stir well to combine. Add chicken, grapes, celery, and red bell pepper. Toss gently. Cover and chill for 2 to 3 hours before serving.

Place pappadum one at a time on paper towel in the microwave. Microwave on high for 45 seconds or until puffed. Set aside. Slice avocados into slices suitable for fanning. Set aside. Using a miniature melon ball cutter, scoop cantaloupe.

TO SERVE: Place pappadum to one side of the plate. Top with chicken salad covering pappadum from middle to one edge. Fan wedges of avocado from edge of chicken salad and place cantaloupe melon balls at juncture of avocado and salad. Sprinkle with macadamia nuts.

5 pounds bone-in chicken breasts

1 (3-inch) piece fresh ginger, sliced
celery tops
1/2 medium onion, cut in wedges
2 bay leaves

1/2 cup mayonnaise
1/2 cup sour cream
1 tablespoon grated fresh ginger
2 teaspoons sugar
grated zest of 1 large lemon
1/2 teaspoon ground ginger
1/2 teaspoon salt

1 cup seedless red grapes, halved
1 cup diced celery
1/2 cup diced red bell pepper

GARNISHES (OPTIONAL)
12 pappadums
2 avocados
1 cantaloupe
1 cup macadamia nuts, toasted

52

Black Bean Confetti Salad

SERVES 8 TO 10

Gently rinse black beans in a sieve and drain well. Rinse corn in sieve and drain well. Combine black beans, corn, bell peppers, onion, and jalapeño pepper.

Make dressing by whisking all ingredients together.

Just before serving, toss together bean mixture, dressing, couscous, and cilantro.

2 (15-ounce) cans of black beans
1 (11-ounce) can whole kernel corn
1/2 cup each minced red and
   green bell pepper
1/4 cup diced purple onion
1 tablespoon finely minced
   jalapeño pepper

1 1/2 cups cooked couscous
1/2 cup cilantro, minced

DRESSING
3 tablespoons fresh squeezed
   lime juice
1/2 cup olive oil
1 clove garlic, minced
2 teaspoons cumin powder
1 teaspoon salt
freshly ground black pepper

Tomatoes & Mozzarella with Fresh Basil Vinaigrette

SERVES 8 TO 10

Place all of the ingredients for the vinaigrette in a food processor and blend until semismooth. Chill for 30 minutes.

Arrange alternating slices of tomato, cheese, and avocado on large flat platter. Top with onion rings. Just before serving, drizzle vinaigrette over salad.

FRESH BASIL VINAIGRETTE
1 cup fresh basil leaves
1 cup olive oil
4 tablespoons red wine vinegar
2 cloves garlic, chopped
1 teaspoon sugar
1 teaspoon salt
1 teaspoon freshly ground
   black pepper

SALAD
4 ripe tomatoes, sliced 1/4 inch thick
1 pound fresh mozzarella,
   sliced 1/4 inch thick
1 avocado, sliced 1/4 inch thick
red onion, sliced thin and separated
   into rings

53

Blue Cheese & Apple Coleslaw

SERVES 16

Using a mandoline, shred cabbage. Core apples. Cut into six pieces and dice into pieces.

In a large bowl, combine cabbage, apples, and blue cheese. Toss gently to combine.

In a separate bowl, combine mayonnaise, sour cream, salt, and pepper. Add to cabbage mixture. Stir to combine. Chill for at least 1 hour before serving.

**3 pounds cabbage
   (12 to 14 cups shredded)
5 or 6 cups sweet apples such as
   Gala or Fuji (about 4 apples)
4 ounces blue cheese, crumbled**

**3/4 cup mayonnaise
3/4 cup sour cream
1 teaspoon salt
freshly ground black pepper**

Asian Spiced Slaw with Fresh Herbs, Garlic & Ginger

SERVES 10 TO 12

In a large mixing bowl, toss together cabbages, green onions, and carrots. Toss in herbs and peanuts.

Whisk together dressing ingredients and pour over cabbage mixture. Serve.

**2 pounds green cabbage, shredded
1 pound purple cabbage, shredded
1 1/2 cups sliced green onions
1 10-ounce bag matchstick carrots**

**1/2 cup fresh basil, chopped
1/2 cup fresh mint, chopped**

1 1/2 cups salted peanuts

**DRESSING
1 cup vegetable oil
2/3 cup rice vinegar
1/4 cup soy sauce
2 teaspoons minced garlic
1 1/2 teaspoons minced fresh ginger**

Roosters Caesar Salad & Dressing

SERVES 6 TO 8

Lemon zest and parsley give a lively freshness to this salad.

DRESSING: In food processor fitted with a steel blade and with machine running, drop garlic through feed tube. Add olive oil and anchovies. Purée. Transfer to mixing bowl and add remaining dressing ingredients. Makes 4 cups.

SALAD: Wash lettuce, break into bite-size pieces, and spin dry. Place in plastic bag and chill for at least 30 minutes. Transfer to salad bowl. Toss with enough dressing to coat. Toss with lemon zest and parsley and serve.

DRESSING
2 large cloves garlic
1/4 cup olive oil
3 ounces anchovies with oil

1 1/2 cups grated Parmesan cheese
1 cup Dijon mustard
2 1/2 cups mayonnaise
1/3 cup lemon juice
1 1/2 tablespoons Worcestershire sauce
1 1/2 teaspoons freshly ground black pepper

SALAD
1 head romaine lettuce
zest of 1 lemon
1/4 cup fresh parsley, chopped

TEACHING NOTES

Roosters Caesar Salad & Dressing

- *Dressing yields more than you will need for salad but stores in refrigerator for 2 to 3 weeks. I frequently use it as a sauce for grilled chicken, seafood, and pasta dishes. It is even good on a baked potato! Don't leave out the anchovies. They add to the flavor without being readily identified.*

- *Want to turn it into more of a main dish salad? . . . Add a piece of grilled salmon or chicken or perhaps sliced hard-boiled eggs and steamed asparagus.*

Salad Greens with Fresh Fruit & Potato Sticks

SERVES 8 TO 12

Just before serving, toss together spinach, lettuce, green onions, oranges, and banana. Drizzle with just enough dressing to coat. Top with potato sticks. Serve immediately.

ORANGE VINAIGRETTE: In a screwtop jar, combine all ingredients and shake to combine. Alternatively, combine in a bowl and whisk.

baby spinach
red tipped lettuce
4 green onions, sliced
2 oranges, peeled and sectioned
1 banana, sliced and quartered

1 can potato sticks

ORANGE VINAIGRETTE
1/4 cup orange juice
1/2 cup olive oil
2 tablespoons sugar
2 tablespoons red wine vinegar
1 tablespoon lemon juice
1 teaspoon Dijon mustard
zest of 1/2 orange
1/2 teaspoon salt

Salad Greens with Fresh Fruit & Potato Sticks

- *In the spring and summer, I add about 1/2 cup chopped fresh mint to this salad dressing. I find that even the fresh mint from the grocery store does not have the intensity of flavor like fresh picked from the garden. Sometimes we just need to enjoy things when they are in season.*

- *Potato sticks have been a grocery store staple for years and are perfect for adding a quick crunch to a salad. Make this recipe more upscale by using the more current multicolored Terra Potato Sticks.*

55

TEACHING NOTES

- *Rice vinegar is less acidic than other vinegars. It is distilled from rice wine (sake). There is pure rice wine vinegar and seasoned rice wine vinegar (less expensive and lesser quality). You can use either in this recipe.*

- *Fried won ton skins are available at your local Chinese take-out. Save yourself the trouble of frying them and pick up a couple of bags.*

- *The Asian ingredients in this recipe are usually available in most large grocery stores. They will cost less if you shop at an ethnic market.*

Kung Pao Salad with Oriental Dressing

MAKES 2¹/₂ CUPS

One of the top three salads at Roosters on the Run!

DRESSING: Combine rice wine vinegar, sesame oil, oyster sauce, honey, hoisin sauce, lime juice, garlic, coriander, and Asian garlic chili sauce in a blender and blend. Remove, add onion and cilantro.

SALAD: Toss lettuces, onions, and peanuts with small amount dressing. Top with won ton skins.

DRESSING
1 cup rice wine vinegar
²/₃ cup oriental sesame oil
¹/₃ cup Asian oyster sauce
¹/₄ cup honey
2 tablespoons hoisin sauce
2 tablespoons lime juice
1 tablespoon minced garlic
2 teaspoons ground coriander
1¹/₂ teaspoons Asian garlic
   chili sauce

¹/₃ cup finely minced red onion
¹/₄ cup fresh cilantro, minced

SALAD
mesclun greens
red-tipped lettuce

green onions, sliced
peanuts
fried won ton skins

Provençal Salad with Mustard Balsamic Vinaigrette

MAKES 2¹/2 TO 3 CUPS

A Roosters on the Run favorite salad with our #1 requested vinaigrette.

VINAIGRETTE: Using an immersion blender or a regular blender, combine all ingredients *except* oil. With blender running, add oil slowly.

Toss together equal parts of romaine and mesclun greens. Top with roasted red pepper pieces and a few kalamatas. Add dressing and toss just to coat. Finish with pieces of goat cheese and toasted almonds.

ROOSTERS MUSTARD BALSAMIC VINAIGRETTE
¹/2 cup Dijon mustard
¹/2 cup balsamic vinegar
¹/3 cup honey
I small clove garlic, minced
¹/2 teaspoon dried thyme
¹/2 teaspoon dried basil
¹/2 teaspoon dried oregano
red pepper flakes to taste

I cup vegetable oil

SALAD
romaine lettuce
mesclun greens

roasted red peppers, cut in strips
kalamata olives, pitted
goat cheese, crumbled
slivered almonds, toasted

TEACHING NOTES

Provençal Salad with Mustard Balsamic Vinaigrette

- *Use a regular or immersion blender for making the vinaigrette. It creates a better emulsion. A food processor could be used but is not my first choice.*

- *Dress salads at the last minute. Do not overdress. Tossing a salad thoroughly will evenly distribute dressing. Too much dressing wilts the salad.*

- *Salads with toppings should be presented in a wide flat bowl. It is easier to toss and ingredients do not settle to the bottom.*

57

TEACHING NOTES

Mixed Greens with Cranberries, Pecans and Blue Cheese Vinaigrette

Toasting nuts brings out their flavor. Salad ingredients are never exact. Adjust amounts according to how many servings are needed. Vinaigrettes and dressings always go further than you expect.

Crunchy Romaine & Parmesan with Lemon Juice Vinaigrette

This crisp, very refreshing salad pairs well with pizzas and rich casseroles. Wash, spin dry, and tear lettuce well ahead of serving time so it has time to crisp up in the refrigerator. For an extra garnish, shave Parmesan cheese curls with a vegetable peeler from a block of Parmesan cheese. Remember when making vinaigrettes that salt really brings out the flavor.

58

Mixed Greens with Cranberries, Pecans and Blue Cheese Vinaigrette

SERVES 6

Toss together salad greens, green onions, dried cranberries, and pecans. In a small bowl, whisk together olive oil and red wine vinegar. Gently whisk in blue cheese. Season with salt and freshly ground black pepper. Toss with greens and serve.

mixed salad greens of choice for
   6 persons
4 green onions, sliced including tops
1/4 cup dried cranberries
1/2 cup pecans, chopped and toasted

VINAIGRETTE
1/2 cup olive oil
3 tablespoons red wine vinegar
1/4 cup blue cheese
1/2 teaspoon salt
freshly ground black pepper

Crunchy Romaine & Parmesan with Lemon Juice Vinaigrette

MAKES 3/4 CUP DRESSING

Trim, wash, and tear lettuce. Set aside.

Combine lemon juice, olive oil, salt, and pepper. Vinaigrette should be very tart. Toss with lettuce and Parmesan cheese. Serve.

1 head romaine
1/4 to 1/2 cup freshly grated Italian
   Parmesan cheese

1/4 cup fresh lemon juice
1/2 cup olive oil
1/2 teaspoon salt
freshly ground black pepper

Honey Dressing

MAKES 1 1/2 CUPS

Simple and straightforward and an old basic to have in your repertoire. This is a good dressing to use when you want to add fruit to your salad. Also good paired with spicier casseroles . . . such as the White Enchiladas (page 97) or Mexican Cornbread Lasagna (page 88).

1/2 cup sugar
1 teaspoon paprika
1 teaspoon dry mustard
1 teaspoon salt
5 tablespoons vinegar
1/3 cup honey
1 cup vegetable oil

Combine all ingredients and whisk together.

SALADS · DRESSINGS

TEACHING NOTES

Honey Dressing

I like to use this salad dressing with a combination of mixed greens. Since this dressing has sugar and honey in it, it can be heavy and crush your greens. If using spinach or a lighter weight green, mix in some romaine or a lettuce that will give some support to your dressing.

Toasted Coriander Vinaigrette

MAKES 1 CUP

In a small sauté pan, toast coriander seeds until fragrant. Keep the pan moving while toasting. In a blender or in the food processor fitted with a steel blade, add toasted seeds and process until ground. Add remaining ingredients and pulse until well combined. Set aside for at least 1 hour for flavors to meld.

1 tablespooon whole coriander seeds

1/4 cup white wine vinegar
3/4 cup olive oil
1/4 teaspoon salt
2 tablespoons cream

TEACHING NOTES

- *Raw almond butter is a jarred product available at organic food stores.*

- *Screwtop jars work great for storage. Just shake and you are ready to go. I know you are saying that the recipe looks too long and involved. Trust me, once you have these 3 jars in your refrigerator, you will realize what a gold mine you have.*

- *Change herbs in vinaigrette according to what you have . . . mix and match. Just remember that parsley and chives mix with most any other herb but basil, tarragon, and dill don't mix well with each other.*

- *And finally, always have a piece of baguette for wiping out the bowl. Yum!*

Xavier's Vinaigrette

MAKES 4 CUPS BASE AND 1 1/2 CUPS VINAIGRETTE

Xavier and I lead tours in Provence. Groups that spend time with us are always clamoring for this recipe at the end of their week. After working with Xavier for 10 years, I think I finally have a written recipe to share. For the hundreds of people who have gone to France with us, this dressing has become a phenomenon.

BASE: Combine the above ingredients and whisk to create an emulsion.

MARINATED ONIONS: Place onions in a 2-cup glass jar. Add enough base to cover. Allow to marinate for several hours before making vinaigrette. Keeps for several weeks refrigerated.

VINAIGRETTE: In a small mixing bowl, combine base and onions. Add red wine vinegar and mustard. Whisk in olive oil. Stir in herbs and salt.

USES: Cook small green beans, drain and chill. Toss with sliced, raw white mushrooms and vinaigrette. Add some extra marinated onions. Serve.

Layer sliced tomatoes, mozzarella, and fresh basil on soft lettuce leaves. Drizzle with vinaigrette. Add hard-boiled egg wedges for a light lunch or dinner.

Steam new potatoes and pass the vinaigrette at the table. Suggest to your guests that they lightly mash their warm potatoes and drizzle with vinaigrette.

Roast or steam fresh beets. Cut into a small dice. Toss with fresh minced parsley and vinaigrette.

BASE
1 1/4 cups fresh lemon juice
2 tablespoons Dijon mustard
1/4 cup raw almond butter
2 1/2 cups grapeseed oil
1 tablespoon salt
freshly ground white pepper

MARINATED ONIONS
2 cups diced onions

VINAIGRETTE
2 tablespoons base
3 tablespoons marinated onions
2 tablespoons red wine vinegar
2 teaspoons Dijon mustard (optional)
3/4 cup olive oil
1/2 cup fresh herbs (parsley, basil, chives, etc.)
1/2 teaspoon salt

Vegetables & Sides ▶

In my home, Thanksgiving has never been about the turkey. It is always about the sides.

MARY JAMES

Vegetables & Sides

at a glance

Roasted Asparagus with Balsamic Glaze

SERVES 8

BALSAMIC GLAZE: Combine vinegar and brown sugar in small saucepan. Bring to a simmer, reduce heat to medium and cook down to a syrupy glaze. Watch carefully. It burns quickly. Cool. Store in refrigerator.

ASPARAGUS: Preheat convection oven to 450 degrees. Cut or snap off the tough ends of the asparagus and discard. For larger asparagus, peel the bottom third or half of each stalk with a vegetable peeler.

Spread asparagus in a single layer on a sheet pan being careful not to crowd them. Drizzle with olive oil and sprinkle with sea salt. Bake in preheated oven until tips begin to roast and brown. Depending on size of asparagus, cooking time could vary from 5 minutes to 15 minutes.

Remove from oven. Drizzle with balsamic glaze and serve.

BALSAMIC GLAZE
1 cup balsamic vinegar
1 tablespoon light brown sugar

ASPARAGUS
2 pounds asparagus
olive oil
Maldon sea salt

TEACHING NOTES

- *Balsamic glaze keeps for months in the refrigerator.*

- *This recipe works best in a convection oven. If using conventional oven, increase heat to 500 degrees.*

- *It is very important not to crowd the pan. Asparagus should roast, not steam.*

- *Use pour spouts in your olive oil and vinegar bottles . . . drizzling becomes more even and much easier!*

TEACHING NOTES

- *This recipe can be done ahead . . . just add the toasted panko at serving time. Otherwise, it becomes soggy.*

- *Serve with grilled meats . . . especially good with lamb.*

Asparagus with Kalamatas & Raspberry Balsamic Vinaigrette

SERVES 8

Snap off tough ends of asparagus. Fill a sauté pan with about 1 inch of water. Bring to a simmer. Add asparagus and cook just until tender and still bright green . . . about 3 to 5 minutes depending on size of asparagus. Remove and chill quickly with an ice bath or very cold water. Pat dry.

Heat olive oil in small fry pan. Add panko and toast lightly, stirring constantly. Remove and add Parmesan cheese. Set aside.

VINAIGRETTE: Whisk together all ingredients.

TO SERVE: Place asparagus on large platter. Drizzle with vinaigrette. Top with olives then toasted panko. Serve room temperature.

2 pounds medium-size
   fresh asparagus

3 tablespoons olive oil
I cup panko (Japanese
   bread crumbs)
1/4 cup Parmesan cheese, grated

1/2 cup kalamata olives, pitted
   and slivered

VINAIGRETTE
3 tablespoons raspberry
   balsamic vinegar
I tablespoon lemon juice
6 or 7 tablespoons olive oil
salt and freshly ground black pepper

Orange-Glazed
Salt-Roasted Beets

SERVES 8

Preheat oven to 325 degrees.

Trim top and bottom of beets. Place upright on sheet pan that has been lined with foil. Cover top of each beet with kosher salt. Cover with second sheet of foil and seal edges into a package. Transfer to preheated oven and bake until tender . . . about 1 hour. Allow to cool. Knock off excess salt. Peel the beets. Cut into 1/2-inch dice.

Combine arrowroot and water. Set aside.

In a small saucepan, combine orange juice, vinegar, and sugar. Bring to a simmer. Whisk in arrowroot mixture to slightly thicken. Stir in beets and cook briefly to glaze.

1 1/2 to 2 pounds medium beets,
   skin on
kosher salt

1 teaspoon arrowroot
1 teaspoon water

1/2 cup freshly squeezed orange juice
1 1/2 teaspoons balsamic vinegar
1 teaspoon sugar

TEACHING NOTES

**Orange-Glazed
Salt-Roasted Beets**

- *Arrowroot has stronger thickening properties than cornstarch and does not thin out when cooked on high heat or reheated. Therefore, it is much better for glazing.*

- *Serve with Pan-Seared Duck Breast (page 113) and Corn Flan (page 66).*

Sweet-&-Sour Cabbage

SERVES 4 TO 6

Shred cabbage into thin shreds. Heat enough olive oil in sauté pan to just cover the bottom. Add cabbage, honey, and red wine vinegar. Cook, stirring occasionally until all the liquid has cooked from the cabbage and the honey and vinegar have evaporated. Continue to cook until there is some carmelization and browning. Season with salt and pepper.

1 pound purple cabbage
olive oil

1/2 cup honey
1/4 cup red wine vinegar

3/4 teaspoon salt
freshly ground black pepper

Sweet-&-Sour Cabbage

There is a balance of sweet with sour in this recipe. If you like it more one way than the other, increase honey or vinegar accordingly. Salt is essential to round out the flavors. Serve with a grilled pork tenderloin.

TEACHING NOTES

Corn Flan

- *Cooking in a water bath keeps the flan from being tough. It cooks more slowly and evenly.*

- *Timbale molds are straight-sided aluminum cups that come in many sizes. Custard cups could be substituted but lack the straight cylindrical shape that presents so well on the plate.*

- *Depending on your menu, dried tarragon could be added to this recipe . . . about 1 teaspoon.*

Creamed Corn

So why a roux? Well, if flour is added directly to a liquid, it will lump. But if you make a roux, you are coating the flour protein so it can be added directly to your sauce or gravy. In my kitchen, there is always a container of roux handy for thickening.

Corn Flan

MAKES 12 (5-OUNCE) TIMBALES

Preheat oven to 350 degrees.

In the food processor fitted with the steel blade, purée the corn with just enough of the cream to create a purée.

In a mixing bowl, whisk eggs. Add corn purée, remaining cream, sugar, salt, and pepper. Whisk to combine.

Fill well buttered timbale molds to within 1/4 inch of the top of the mold. Place molds in flat roasting pan with sides. Transfer to preheated oven. Add enough water to rise 1 inch up side of molds. Bake for 30 to 35 minutes or until set. When done, lift molds from water bath using tongs. Run knife around edge to unmold.

3 cups frozen sweet yellow corn (1 pound), thawed

2 cups cream
6 eggs
1 1/2 tablespoons sugar
1 teaspoon salt
white pepper to taste

Creamed Corn

MAKES 2 QUARTS

Customers flocked to the deli counter for creamed corn. Some customers ordered 10 and 12 quarts at a time. That is called stocking the freezer!

ROUX: To make roux, melt 1/2 cup butter in saucepan. Add 1/2 cup flour. Cook for 3 to 4 minutes, stirring constantly. Do not allow to brown. Transfer to storage container and refrigerate. Use as needed to thicken soups, sauces, etc.

CREAMED CORN: In food processor fitted with a steel blade, pulse half of the corn to a coarse texture. Do not over-process. Transfer to 3- or 4-quart saucepan. Add water and cream. Bring to a boil. Add 3 tablespoons roux. Stir to incorporate and cook until thickened. Simmer, stirring frequently for 10 to 15 minutes. Add remaining corn. Cook for another 5 minutes. Season to taste with salt and freshly ground black pepper.

ROUX
1/2 cup butter
1/2 cup flour

CREAMED CORN
2 pounds frozen corn, divided
1 1/2 cups water
2 cups heavy cream

3 tablespoons roux

2 teaspoons salt
freshly ground black pepper to taste

Braised Fennel

SERVES 4 TO 6

Trim fennel by cutting off the leafy upper stalks and just a very thin slice from bottom. Remove any tough or scarred outer pieces. Cut each bulb lengthwise in half, and quarter if bulbs are large.

In a heavy sauté pan, heat olive oil and butter. Place fennel, cut side down, in pan. Season with salt and pepper. Sear until golden. Turn to sear each side. Once browned, add chicken stock to come halfway up sides of fennel. Cover and simmer until tender . . . about 15 minutes. Check for tenderness with the tip of a knife. Remove cover, increase heat to high and reduce stock to a glaze. Remove from heat. Continue in sauté pan or transfer to ovenproof gratin dish. Top with desired cheese. Place in preheated 375-degree oven to melt cheese. Or place under broiler to melt cheese.

3 bulbs fennel
salt and freshly ground black pepper

2 tablespoons olive oil
1/2 tablespoon butter

chicken stock
fresh Parmesan, Comté, or cantal
  cheese, grated

Le Puy Lentils

SERVES 8

Le Puy lentils come from the Auvergne region of France and are high on my comfort food list. Perfect with duck leg confit.

Wash lentils in several changes of water. In a large saucepan, heat duck fat and sauté onion, celery, and carrots until tender. Add lentils, and then stock to cover by 1 to 2 inches. Bring to a simmer and cook for 20 to 30 minutes or tender. Drain if necessary.

2 cups lentils, preferably green lentils
  from Le Puy

duck fat or olive oil
1 cup chopped purple onion
1/2 cup chopped celery
1 cup finely diced carrots

duck, chicken, or vegetable stock

TEACHING NOTES

Braised Fennel

- *Sometimes you have the perfect pan or dish for a particular recipe. For me, I have a copper gratin pan with a lid. It works great on top of the stove and can go to the oven and then the table. Love it. Only one pan to wash. Sometimes it is the little things that make life in the kitchen more pleasant!*

- *Fennel can be done ahead. If it is cold, just reheat in oven until hot. Reheats beautifully.*

Le Puy Lentils

No need to soak lentils, a good rinsing is all that is necessary. Be careful not to overcook. Too many people put these into the dried bean category and think they need to be cooked for hours. Lentils should be tender with a slight bite and you should be able to separate them with a fork.

TEACHING NOTES

- Use a mushroom brush or paper towel to clean mushroom caps.

- Stuffed mushrooms can be completed ahead and reheated in the oven or microwave.

- To make fresh bread crumbs, process stale bread, usually a baguette, in food processor.

- Gruyère or even Emmenthaler Swiss could be substituted for the Comté.

Stuffed Mushrooms

SERVES 8

These big mushrooms can be served as a side with meats but are also good as a side to a lunchtime salad.

Carefully remove stems from mushrooms and finely chop. Reconstitute porcini mushrooms in boiling water; drain well and finely chop.

In a 10-inch sauté pan, heat olive oil, add mushroom stems and porcini mushrooms. Cook until liquid from mushrooms is evaporated. Season with salt and pepper. Add marsala and again cook until evaporated. Stir in bread crumbs, garlic, and thyme. Set aside to cool.

Once cooled, add Comté cheese. Press filling into mushroom caps. Place on baking sheet. Drizzle with olive oil and a grind of fresh black pepper. Bake in preheated 375-degree oven for 30 to 45 minutes.

VARIATION: Dice 4 slices raw bacon and cook until crisp. Set aside. Drain fat from skillet and proceed with recipe. Add cooked bacon when adding bread crumbs.

18 large white mushrooms

1/2 cup dried porcini mushrooms
3 tablespoons olive oil
reserved stems, chopped
salt and freshly ground black pepper

1/4 cup dry or sweet marsala
    (or dry sherry)

1 1/2 cups fresh bread crumbs
2 cloves garlic, minced
3/4 teaspoon dried thyme

1 cup grated Comté cheese

olive oil

Parmesan Green Bell Pepper Rings

SERVES 6 TO 8

These are a hit every time they are served. Perfect with steaks from the grill or as an appetizer. Even if you think you don't like green peppers, you will love these green pepper rings.

Slice peppers into $1/4$- to $1/2$-inch-thick slices. Remove seeds. In 3 separate bowls, combine bread crumbs and cheese. Set aside. Combine eggs and milk. Set aside. Combine flour and black pepper. Set aside.

Set up assembly line with bowls of 3 mixtures. First dip rings into milk mixture, then flour mixture, back to milk mixture, then into bread crumb/cheese mixture. Place on sheet pan until ready to fry.

TO FRY: Using a deep-fat fryer or a wok, heat 2 to 3 cups vegetable oil to 375 degrees. Fry several rings at a time until golden brown. Transfer to paper towel-lined pan.

VARIATION: To make onion rings, slice one very large yellow onion into $1/4$-inch-thick rings. Omit the cheese in the bread crumbs.

2 or 3 large green bell peppers

1 $1/3$ cups seasoned bread crumbs
$1/2$ cup grated Parmesan cheese

2 eggs
2 cups milk

2 cups flour
freshly ground black pepper

2 to 3 cups vegetable oil for frying

TEACHING NOTES

- *The bread crumbs for this recipe are commercially prepared, already seasoned fine bread crumbs available in grocery stores. When breading pepper rings, concentrate on keeping one hand dry (flour and bread crumbs) and the other hand can be used for dipping in the milk/egg mixture. Rings can be breaded early in the day, ready for frying just before serving.*

- *To freeze breaded pepper rings, fry partially, do not allow to brown. Drain. Place on sheet pan. Freeze, and then bag. Finish frying just before serving.*

69

TEACHING NOTES

- *There is really no substitute for fresh nutmeg. It keeps forever as opposed to the powdered in the can. The microplane grater is the perfect tool for grating nutmeg. This tool is indispensable in the kitchen . . . perfect for zests, hard cheeses, and nutmeg.*

- *Don't worry about a little sticking on bottom of pan when potatoes are simmering. If you have some sticking or scorching, just leave that behind when you transfer to the gratin dishes.*

- *It is just as easy to do 5 pounds of potatoes as 2 1/2 pounds. The leftovers are fabulous for breakfast!*

Potatoes Gratin

SERVES 12 TO 16

Potatoes Gratin was always a part of a holiday dinner class that Harrison Turner and I taught each November. It is the classic accompaniment to beef tenderloin.

Peel potatoes and slice 1/8 inch thick using a mandoline. Put into a large saucepan or stockpot with milk. Bring to a boil and simmer for about 15 minutes. In a separate saucepan, bring the cream to a simmer. When potatoes have come to a simmer, add hot cream. Cook together for 4 to 5 minutes. Potatoes are not cooked at this point. While potatoes are simmering, use a rubber spatula to gently lift potatoes off the bottom of the pan being careful to keep potato slices intact.

Heavily butter two 3-quart gratin or casserole dishes and sprinkle with minced garlic. Add potatoes in layers, seasoning with salt, pepper, and nutmeg as you layer. Finally, pour remaining milk and cream mixture over the potatoes. Dot with butter and bake at 400 degrees for 1 hour or until brown and bubbly.

5 pounds baking potatoes
1 quart whole milk
2 cups heavy cream

1 tablespoon butter
2 large cloves garlic, minced

salt and freshly ground black pepper
freshly grated nutmeg

2 to 3 tablespoons butter

Parmesan-Cheddar Twice-Baked Potatoes

MAKES 16

These extremely popular potatoes were a staple in the Roosters on the Run case. Keep them on hand in your freezer.

Preheat oven to 375 degrees. Bake potatoes for 45 minutes to 1 hour or until fork tender. Remove from oven and cool for 15 minutes. Slice potatoes into equal halves horizontally. Carefully scoop out potato and place in mixing bowl. Add butter. Mix briefly. Add milk to achieve desired consistency then add Cheddar cheese, Parmesan cheese, salt, and pepper. Mix just to combine. Do not overmix. Fill potato skins with mixture and top with grated Cheddar cheese.

TO SERVE: Reheat potatoes in 350-degree oven for 20 to 30 minutes or until hot through.

8 Idaho baking potatoes
1/2 cup butter
1 1/4 cups milk
3/4 cup grated sharp Cheddar cheese
1/4 cup grated Parmesan cheese
2 teaspoons salt
1/2 teaspoon freshly ground
   black pepper

GARNISH
1 1/2 cups grated sharp
   Cheddar cheese

TEACHING NOTES

- *The basic mashed potato is simple if you remember one cardinal rule. Do not overbeat! Once overbeaten, the starch in the potato changes, and they become like wallpaper paste. Sadly, there is nothing you can do to retrieve them at this point.*

- *Since the size of potatoes varies, milk measurement may not be exact. Be flexible.*

- *If freezing potatoes, add cheese topping at time of serving.*

TEACHING NOTES

- *Unlike white potatoes, sweet potatoes should never be baked above 375 degrees. It changes the starch structure of the potato.*

- *This recipe can be done ahead and frozen. If it is going to be frozen, do not add the final layer of apples. Add apples just before baking.*

- *Apples are shredded before puréeing potatoes so that the food processor bowl will not have to be washed . . . a time saver.*

- *If potatoes are too stiff . . . add more bourbon!*

- *The number of servings is difficult to ascertain since it is usually part of a huge Thanksgiving buffet and there are so many other side dishes. But, then again, aren't leftovers great.*

Sweet Potato-Apple Casserole

SERVES 8

The apples in this dish are a refreshing change from the marshmallow-topped sweet potato casseroles so often seen at Thanksgiving.

Preheat oven to 375 degrees. Bake the potatoes for approximately 1 hour or until tender when pierced with a knife. Cool slightly.

In food processor fitted with a grating blade, shred apples. Remove and set aside.

Remove skins from potatoes and discard. In food processor fitted with a steel blade, add potato pulp, butter, corn syrup, brown sugar, bourbon, cinnamon, nutmeg, and salt. Purée until smooth, scraping down side of bowl as necessary.

Butter a 3-quart flat casserole or gratin dish. Spread half of the puréed mixture in the prepared dish. Add half the shredded apples. Add remaining potatoes and finish with remaining apples. Sprinkle with brown sugar and drizzle with butter. Bake at 375 degrees until hot . . . about 30 minutes.

6 medium sweet potatoes
2 or 3 Granny Smith apples, peeled and cored

6 tablespoons butter
1/4 cup dark corn syrup
1/4 cup dark brown sugar
2 tablespoons bourbon
1 teaspoon cinnamon
freshly grated nutmeg
salt

3 or 4 tablespoons brown sugar
2 tablespoons butter

Seared Spinach with Pine Nuts

SERVES 6

Wash spinach. Remove larger stems. Lightly spin dry . . . you want some water still clinging to the leaves.

In a wok or large sauté pan, heat olive oil. Add spinach. Cover to wilt. Then uncover, use tongs to lift and toss. Increase heat to high and continue to cook until liquid is evaporated. Remove. It may be necessary to do this in two batches.

In the same pan, heat 1 tablespoon olive oil, add shallots and sauté until tender. Add pine nuts, and then spinach. Season with salt and grate a bit of nutmeg over all. Serve.

2¹/₂ pounds spinach
2 tablespoons olive oil

1 tablespoon olive oil
2 shallots, chopped
¹/₃ cup pine nuts, toasted
Maldon sea salt
fresh nutmeg

TEACHING NOTES

- *There are so many variations of this recipe. Substitute spinach with Swiss chard or kale. Toasted walnuts can be used instead of pine nuts.*

- *Maldon sea salt is a flaky salt that is a favorite for finishing vegetables and meats. If you don't have it, use kosher salt.*

- *Nuts can be toasted in a dry skillet or on a sheet pan in a 350-degree oven. Cooking time will vary depending on the freshness of your nuts. Watch carefully and stir occasionally.*

- *The wok is the ideal pan for searing greens. And yes, 2¹/2 pounds only serves 6 people.*

- *Cook the spinach ahead but finish with nuts, shallots, and seasoning just before serving. Reheat the spinach in the microwave before tossing with shallot mixture.*

73

TEACHING NOTES

- *This is a unique side dish for salads and soups. To seed tomatoes, cut tomato in half horizontally, squeeze over sink using your fingertips to remove seeds.*

- *In winter, buy the vine-ripened tomatoes that still have the vine attached.*

- *This pastry dough is very easy to work with. To ease transfer to skillet, fold rolled out pastry in half and place over tomatoes, unfold and tuck edges.*

- *To do recipe ahead, transfer cooked tart from skillet as directed and set aside on sheet pan until ready to reheat.*

- *Variations abound. Add a few oil-cured olives just before covering tomatoes with pastry. Fresh basil can be added at this time if desired. Use flavored oils such as rosemary or garlic instead of olive oil.*

Tomato Tarte Tatin

SERVES 8

This recipe was inspired by a popular first course at L'Autre Côté du Lavoir, a favorite restaurant in Provence.

DOUGH: In food processor fitted with a steel blade, process flour, butter, egg white, cheese, pepper, and salt until the texture of coarse crumbs. With the machine still running, add 2 to 3 tablespoons chilled water and process just until mixture presses together with your fingertips. Remove from processor, press into round disk. Wrap in plastic wrap.

In a 8½- to 9-inch ovenproof skillet, heat the oil and butter. Add the sugar and heat until it begins to brown and caramelize. Pack the tomatoes cut side down into the pan and season with salt and pepper. Cook over high heat for a few minutes until the tomatoes are soft and begin to color on the undersides. Using a narrow offset icing spatula, carefully turn tomatoes one at a time. Cook briefly to finish evaporating most of pan juices. Remove from the heat.

Preheat the oven to 400 degrees. Roll out the dough on a lightly floured surface until it is slightly larger than the skillet. Put the dough over the tomatoes and tuck the edges down the sides. Bake for 20 minutes or until the pastry is golden. Remove from the heat and leave to cool for about 5 minutes so the juices can settle. Invert onto a plate so the pastry is on the bottom.

DOUGH

1 cup all-purpose flour
4 tablespoons butter, in 4 pieces
1 egg white
½ cup grated Parmesan or
    Romano cheese
¾ teaspoon fresh coarsely ground
    black pepper
pinch of salt
2 to 3 tablespoons chilled water

1 tablespoon olive oil
1 tablespoon butter
2 teaspoons sugar
6 tomatoes, halved crosswise, seeded
salt and pepper

Vegetable Gratin

A colorful addition to your summer table.

ONIONS: In a large sauté pan, heat olive oil and add onions. Cook slowly until brown and caramelized. This can take 20 to 30 minutes. Deglaze with 1 to 2 tablespoons of water 1 or 2 times to facilitate caramelization.

VEGETABLES: Slice tomatoes 1/4 inch thick. Set aside. Slice zucchini and yellow squash on the diagonal 1/4 inch thick. Set aside. Peel eggplant if desired. Cut into slices about the same size as squashes.

Gently combine all the vegetables in a large bowl. Drizzle with olive oil and toss with 1 cup Parmesan cheese and 2 teaspoons of chosen seasoning.

ASSEMBLY: Place caramelized onions evenly across the bottom of a 3-quart gratin dish or casserole. Arrange overlapping slices of the four vegetables in rows alternating the vegetables i.e., yellow squash, tomato, zucchini, and eggplant until all are used (stand veggies on edge as much as possible) or casserole is full. Drizzle lightly with olive oil. Combine 1/2 cup Parmesan cheese and herbes de Provence. Sprinkle over the top of the vegetables.

TO COOK: Bake in preheated 375-degree oven until well browned and vegetables are tender . . . about 1 hour.

ONIONS
2 tablespoons olive oil
2 pounds yellow onions, thinly sliced
1 to 2 tablespoons water

VEGETABLES
1 1/2 pounds Roma tomatoes
1 pound zucchini
1 pound yellow squash
1 small eggplant

olive oil
1 cup grated Parmesan cheese
2 teaspoons Italian seasoning or herbes de Provence

1/4 to 1/2 cup Parmesan cheese
1 teaspoon Italian seasoning or herbes de Provence

TEACHING NOTES

- *Don't let the length of the recipe deter you; it is just a concept that really needs no recipe after the first time.*

- *Change the vegetables being careful that all will cook at the same rate. Or add some feta cheese while layering vegetables. Or change the seasoning blend. Or add fresh herbs such as basil leaves.*

TEACHING NOTES

- *Any vegetables can be chosen. However, you must think about the cooking time of each. If you choose a hard root vegetable, it will take longer to cook than a softer vegetable. So cut it smaller. Other choices might be turnips, parsnips, mushrooms, and butternut squash. This recipe yields about 20 cups of raw vegetables that become 6 to 8 cups when cooked.*

- *Always make more than you need for one meal. They reheat great in microwave.*

- *Obviously, you will have more spice than needed for one recipe. It stores indefinitely. We used this mixture on the salad croutons at Roosters on the Run.*

- *And finally, this recipe is one that absolutely calls for a convection oven. Vegetables just wilt in a regular oven. Grilling in a grill basket would be an alternative.*

Roasted Vegetables with Veggie Spice Rub

SERVES 8 TO 10

Preheat convection oven to 425 degrees.

Combine veggie spices. Stir well. Store in glass jar.

Prep vegetables. (Twenty cups of raw vegetables yield 6 to 8 cups roasted vegetables).

In a large mixing bowl, toss vegetables with olive oil. Sprinkle with Veggie Spice Rub. Toss again. Spread in a single layer on two 11×17×1-inch sheet pans and roast in preheated oven for 45 minutes. Stir occasionally.

VEGGIE SPICE RUB
1/4 cup kosher salt
2 tablespoons cracked black pepper
2 tablespoons dried thyme
2 tablespoons dried oregano
1 1/2 teaspoons dried basil
1 1/2 tablespoons garlic powder
1 tablespoon onion powder

VEGETABLES
1 medium eggplant, cut into
   2-inch chunks
1 red bell pepper, cut into
   2-inch pieces
1 yellow bell pepper, cut into
   2-inch pieces
1 green bell pepper, cut into
   2-inch pieces
2 yellow squash, cut into chunks
2 medium zucchini, cut into chunks
1 large onion, cut into wedges
   and separated
1 sweet potato, cut into 1- to
   2-inch cubes
2 carrots, cut into 1-inch pieces

1/3 to 1/2 cup olive oil
1 1/2 tablespoons Veggie Spice Rub

Cornbread Sausage Dressing

MAKES 24 (3-INCH) PATTIES

Dressing patties are perfect for the do-ahead cook. And the cornbread recipe will be one you will use over and over.

Melt butter in skillet. Sauté onion and celery until soft and translucent. Set aside.

Combine cornbread and stuffing mix. Toss with salt and pepper. Add cooled vegetables. Add eggs and sausage, combining well. Add chicken stock to achieve a fairly mushy mixture but it should still hold together. Stir in baking powder and sage. Thin with more chicken stock if necessary. The amount of chicken stock necessary is dependent upon the staleness of the cornbread . . . several cups are usually needed.

Shape into patties making an indentation (for a touch of gravy before serving) in the center. Bake for 30 to 40 minutes at 350 degrees.

CORNBREAD: Preheat the oven to 425 degrees. Combine cornmeal, egg, and shortening. Add buttermilk to achieve a batter consistency. Let stand for 5 to 10 minutes and add more buttermilk to return mixture to batter-like consistency.

Preheat 10-inch skillet on top of stove. Add 2 to 3 tablespoons fat (bacon, oil, or butter). When very hot, pour batter into pan and transfer to preheated oven to bake for 20 to 25 minutes.

2 or 3 tablespoons butter
1 large onion, chopped
1 1/2 cups chopped celery
1 recipe stale crumbled cornbread
1 (8-ounce) bag Pepperidge Farm
    herb-seasoned stuffing
salt and pepper
2 eggs
1 pound Neese's Country Sausage
    (mild, hot, or extra sage),
    uncooked
chicken stock
1 teaspoon baking powder
1 tablespoon dry sage

CORNBREAD
2 cups self-rising white cornmeal
1 egg
3 to 4 tablespoons shortening or
    bacon fat, melted
buttermilk
2 to 3 tablespoons bacon fat,
    oil, or butter

TEACHING NOTES

- *Make the cornbread 2 to 3 days ahead of when you are making the dressing. Crumble and leave uncovered so it will become stale. Dressing patties can be frozen on a cookie sheet then removed and bagged in freezer until ready to use. Remove from bag while they are still frozen and place on baking sheet. Thaw. Bake as directed.*

- *Neese's Country Sausage is a Greensboro, North Carolina, product that I swear by . . . yes, swear by it. It has a great flavor with not too much fat. If not available in your area, it can be purchased on their Web site www.neesesausage.com.*

77

TEACHING NOTES

Lemony Orzo with Olives and Fresh Basil

- *To chiffonade an herb, stack the leaves, choosing the two largest leaves for the top and bottom of the stack. Roll up tightly like a cigar and slice into very thin slices. Once sliced, take knife and make 3 cuts across the slices. Voila! You have perfectly cut herbs. Basil bruises and turns black if it is chopped*

- *Orzo/riso will have a better consistency on the plate when it is returned to the hot pan after being drained. This evaporates any remaining water and helps the dish to hold together.*

- *Using a variety of olives adds interest and is important to the dish.*

- *If you don't have Minor's base, use chicken or vegetable stock instead of water*

- *Can be done ahead and reheated in microwave.*

Creamy Cheesy Grits   SERVES 6 TO 8

In a 2-quart saucepan, combine milk, grits, and salt. Bring to a simmer and cook until milk is absorbed. Remove from heat and stir in butter, Worcestershire sauce, hot sauce, cheese, and sherry. Stir in beaten egg. Pour into a greased 2-quart baking dish. Top with remaining 1/2 cup cheese.

Bake at 300 degrees for 1 hour or until bubbly.

4 cups milk
1 cup quick-cooking grits
1 1/2 teaspoons salt

4 tablespoons butter
1 1/2 teaspoons Worcestershire sauce
1 1/2 teaspoons Texas Pete hot sauce or hot pepper sauce
1 cup grated extra-sharp Cheddar cheese
1 tablespoon dry sherry
1 egg, beaten

1/2 cup grated extra-sharp Cheddar cheese

Lemony Orzo with Olives and Fresh Basil   SERVES 8

Bring water to a boil. Stir in chicken base. Add orzo. Cover and simmer until tender . . . about 10 to 15 minutes. Drain, if necessary. Return to pan over low heat for less than a minute just to evaporate any lingering water.

While orzo is cooking, combine olives, olive oil, lemon zest and juice, basil, and green onions. Toss with warm orzo. Season with salt and pepper. Serve.

8 to 10 cups water
2 tablespoons Minor's chicken or vegetable base
2 cups orzo or riso

1/2 cup oil-cured olives, pitted and chopped
1/2 cup picholine olives, pitted and chopped
1/4 cup olive oil
zest and juice of 1 lemon
1/3 cup fresh basil, chiffonade
3 green onions, chopped
salt and freshly ground pepper to taste

Wild Rice with Brown Butter

SERVES 8

Rinse rice thoroughly. Bring water to a boil Add wild rice. Reduce heat to gentle boil and cover tightly.

Cook just until tender (approximately 1 hour). Rice is done when grains have "popped" and begin to curl. Drain any excess liquid if necessary. Fluff with a fork and serve with browned butter.

TO BROWN BUTTER: Heat $1/2$ cup salted butter in 2 cup measuring cup for 3 to 4 minutes on High in the microwave. Butter is ready when it is a nutty brown. Or heat in small skillet until browned.

2 cups wild rice

5 cups water

1 teaspoon salt

BROWN BUTTER

$1/2$ cup salted butter

TEACHING NOTES

Wild Rice with Brown Butter

- *This recipe can be done 2 or 3 days ahead. Cover with plastic wrap and reheat in microwave. Freezes well with or without the butter.*

- *For Green Beans Almondine, add sliced almonds to butter just before the butter begins to brown and then pour over lightly steamed green beans.*

- *Brown Butter is also a quick topping for steamed broccoli, asparagus, or potatoes.*

Roosters Macaroni & Cheese

SERVES 6 TO 8

Oh my goodness, how much of this did Roosters on the Run sell?

Bring a large pot of water to a boil. Add macaroni and cook until tender. Drain thoroughly.

In a 3-quart saucepan, melt butter. Add flour and cook for 1 to 2 minutes. Add milk, whisking vigorously to incorporate. Add salt and pepper.

ASSEMBLY: Layer half of the cooked macaroni in a 2-quart flat casserole. Add half the white sauce. Top with 2 cups Cheddar cheese. Add final layer of macaroni and remainder of white sauce. Finish with final $1/2$ cup of grated Cheddar cheese.

Bake in preheated 400-degree oven for 30 to 35 minutes or until top is golden.

3 cups elbow macaroni

$1/4$ cup butter
$1/4$ cup flour
$2 1/4$ cups milk
1 teaspoon salt
freshly ground black pepper

$2 1/2$ cups grated extra-sharp Cheddar cheese

Roosters Macaroni & Cheese

Really good extra-sharp cheese is the key to this recipe. Roosters always used an aged 2 year old Cheddar. Kraft Cracker Barrel Extra-Sharp Cheddar will work. As a rule, the store brands of extra-sharp Cheddar are not sharp enough.

TEACHING NOTES

Cranberry Conserve

- *Cooking time is accurate. Mixture will appear too thin but it sets up upon cooling. You still want to see the pieces of fruit. This recipe is great for gift giving and can be doubled. Do not do more than a double batch. It does not cook and set up properly.*

- *Serve in a glass bowl. This adds great color to your table. It is also good as an addition to the next day's turkey sandwiches.*

Spiced Oranges with Grand Marnier

Make sure oranges are submerged in syrup. The longer the oranges stay in the syrup, the more flavorful they are.

Cranberry Conserve

MAKES 1½ QUARTS

I taught a 'Southern Thanksgiving' class at least 2 or 3 times each year. And this was one of the most popular dishes in the class. It is just not Thanksgiving without this colorful dish on the table.

In a 4- or 5- quart saucepan, cook cranberries in water until skins begin to pop . . . just 2 or 3 minutes. Add sugar and stir. Squeeze lemon and orange juice into cranberries (use a strainer to catch the seeds). Add squeezed lemon and orange halves, raisins, apple, pear, and apricots. Bring to a boil, reduce heat and cook for 15 to 20 minutes. Remove from heat. Using tongs, remove lemon and orange halves and discard. Stir in port and walnuts and let cool to room temperature. Chill.

4 cups fresh cranberries
1 cup water

2½ cups sugar
1 lemon
1 orange

1 cup raisins
1 apple, cored, diced
1 pear, cored, diced
½ cup dried apricots, cut in quarters

⅓ cup port wine
1 cup walnuts, coarsely chopped

Spiced Oranges with Grand Marnier

SERVES 12 TO 16

Excellent accompaniment to brunch menus.

Using a vegetable peeler, remove just the peel of 3 oranges. Try not to get any of the white pith with the peel. Cut peel into slivers. Set aside.

Now remove all the peel and pith from all the oranges (pith from 3 and peel and pith from 7). Slice into ¼-inch slices. Place in large glass or ceramic bowl.

In a large saucepan, combine sugar, water, cinnamon sticks, cloves, and slivered orange peel. Bring to a boil and cook for 8 to 10 minutes or until slightly thickened. Add Grand Marnier. Turn off heat. Add orange slices. Cool. Refrigerate for several days before serving.

10 navel oranges

2½ cups sugar
1¼ cups water
3 (3-inch) cinnamon sticks
8 to 10 whole cloves

3 to 4 tablespoons Grand Marnier

Smoked Pepper Butter MAKES 1/2 POUND

Halve the bell peppers and remove seeds.

STOVETOP SMOKER METHOD:
Using 1 tablespoon hickory dust, smoke the peppers cut side down in the Cameron smoker for 10 to 15 minutes or until smoke has subsided. Remove and set aside to cool. Cut into small dice. Proceed with recipe.

WOK METHOD FOR SMOKING:
Line wok with heavy duty aluminum foil extending foil at least 4 to 5 inches beyond edge of wok. Place a smoking mixture of 1/3 cup long grain rice, 2 tablespoons loose black tea, and 2 tablespoons light brown sugar in bottom of wok. Place a round cake rack or steaming rack in wok so it is 2 or 3 inches above mixture. Place peppers cut side down on rack. Turn on heat and at the first whisp of smoke, cover with lid and pull foil up around edges of lid to seal. Reduce heat. Smoke peppers for 10 to 15 minutes.

TO MAKE BUTTER: In food processor fitted with a steel blade, process butter, lime zest, lime juice, and pepper. Remove, and by hand, stir in approximately 1/4 cup diced smoked peppers. Use the remaining peppers as a "confetti" garnish on the plate.

Slice into 1/4-inch slices and serve over hot grilled beef, chicken, or fish.

1 1/2 bell peppers
   (use a combination of colors)

1 cup butter
zest of 1 lime
2 to 3 teaspoons lime juice
freshly ground black pepper

VEGETABLES · SIDES

TEACHING NOTES

- *I know, I know . . . you are saying this is too much trouble. But it can be done ahead. It can be frozen (butter only, not the garnish). And it is really simple if you have a Cameron Smoker. This simple indoor stovetop smoker can be used for meat, fish, or vegetables. Try smoking corn to add to corn cakes or corn fritters . . . yum, yum.*

- *If you are not a person who likes to make sauces, this is an excellent accompaniment to grilled chicken, beef, or pork. It also works extremely well with grilled or steamed fish. So on a rainy day, stock your freezer.*

81

TEACHING NOTES

Don't panic at the number of garlic cloves. It is correct. Use this butter on steaks, chops, vegetables, and even pizzas.

Xavier's Garlic Butter

MAKES 1 POUND

If we think of the 'trinity' of Xavier's cooking, it has to include his garlic butter, his vinaigrette, and his tapenade, and if we could add a fourth, it would be his aïoli. So many things are done with each of them.

Remove paper skin from garlic cloves. Split each garlic clove in half and remove sprout from center. Wash and spin parsley dry. Remove large stems leaving mostly leaves.

In food processor fitted with a steel blade, purée garlic and parsley. Add butter, salt, basil, and freshly ground black pepper. Purée until well combined. Remove from food processor and place on plastic wrap and roll into 1- to 2-inch cylinders. Store in freezer.

3/4 cup garlic cloves
2 bunches parsley

1 pound butter, room temperature
2 teaspoons salt
1 teaspoon dry basil or
   1/4 cup fresh basil
freshly ground black pepper

Meat, Poultry & Seafood

▶ *. . . the centerpiece of your plate,*
the focus of your attention . . . .

MARY JAMES

Meat, Poultry & Seafood

at a glance

Beef Tenderloin with Stilton & Port Sauce

SERVES 8

Trim tenderloin removing fat, silver skin, and chain. Butterfly the beef tenderloin by cutting beef lengthwise down the center about two-thirds of the way through the beef. Open and begin to flatten. Make at least two more cuts on each side of the first cut, continuing to open like a book. Meat should be fairly flat and open.

Crumble Stilton and place down the center of the butterflied meat. Season with salt and freshly ground black pepper. Bring edges together and tie with butcher twine. Tuck tail and tie to make a more even piece of meat.

In a large ovenproof sauté pan, sear beef in oil and butter. Place in preheated 450-oven for 20 minutes or until thermometer registers 125 to 130 degrees for medium rare. Remove from oven and let rest for 5 to 10 minutes before slicing.

PORT SAUCE: In a heavy-bottomed saucepan, heat oil over medium heat; add carrot, celery, mushrooms, and shallot. Sauté until golden. Add flour and cook slowly for 2 or 3 minutes. Add bay leaf, tarragon, demi-glace, water, port, and salt. Simmer until reduced by about half and sauce lightly coats a spoon. Adjust seasonings. Strain using a fine strainer or chinois. Whisk in butter, 1 tablespoon at a time. Do not overheat once butter is added.

1 tenderloin of beef
8 ounces Stilton cheese
salt and freshly ground black pepper
clarified butter and olive oil
    for sautéeing

PORT SAUCE
1 tablespoon vegetable oil
1 carrot, chopped
1 celery stalk, chopped
1/3 cup mushrooms, chopped
1 shallot, chopped

2 tablespoons flour

1 bay leaf
1/2 teaspoon dried tarragon
1.5-ounces More Than Gourmet
    demi-glace
2 cups water
2 cups port
3/4 to 1 teaspoon salt
4 tablespoons butter, chilled

TEACHING NOTES

To clarify butter, melt 1/2 cup butter. The milk solids will separate. Pour off the clear liquid; this is the clarified butter. Discard solids.

85

TEACHING NOTES

- *Buy a roast that is 2 inches thick. It will cook better than the thinner roasts which tend to dry out.*

- *Pot roast is always better if cooked early in the day and allowed to cool off in its juices before reheating and serving.*

- *Ideally, I prefer to cook a pot roast a day ahead. Place the meat and vegetables in an ovenproof casserole or large gratin dish and the gravy/pan juices in a bowl. Refrigerate both. After refrigeration, the fat from the gravy/pan juices can be easily removed. Then pour over roast and reheat everything in preheated 350-degree oven for 20 to 30 minutes. If serving immediately, use a fat separator and pour off gravy leaving fat behind.*

Pot Roast

SERVES 4

The most basic version of comforting pot roast.

Coat meat heavily with flour. Season with salt and pepper.

On the stovetop, heat oil in a 6- or 7-quart heavy-bottomed ovenproof casserole or Dutch oven. Add meat and sear to brown well on both sides. Add vegetables. Add broth and bay leaves. Bring to a simmer. Cover and transfer to preheated 350-degree oven and cook for 2 to 2½ hours.

When meat is done, it will easily pull apart when pierced with a fork and the broth will have slightly thickened into a gravy.

TO SERVE: Lift meat from gravy and place on platter surrounded by vegetables. Top with gravy.

1 (4-pound) boneless chuck roast
¼ cup flour
salt and freshly ground black pepper

3 to 4 tablespoons vegetable oil
4 carrots, cut into 2-inch pieces
2 pounds red potatoes, trimmed and cut into chunks
1 medium onion, cut into 1-inch pieces

3 cups beef broth
2 bay leaves

Beef Barbecue

Great on a bun, over egg noodles, or by itself. This recipe was always taken along on beach and ski trips.

Cut beef into large chunks. Place into 6- or 7-quart ovenproof casserole. Add vegetables, beef broth, dry mustard, and chili powder. Cover. Bake in preheated 350-degree oven for 3 hours. Remove from oven and let cool for 1 hour.

Lift meat from casserole. When cool enough to handle, pull apart with forks or your fingers. Remove and discard the vegetables. Return meat to casserole with only ¹/2 cup of pan juices. Add BBQ sauce and bring to a simmer on top of the stove. Cook for 20 to 30 minutes over medium heat. Stir occasionally, just lifting meat off bottom of pan. Be gentle or meat will loose its texture.

Serve on toasted buns or over egg noodles.

- 1 (7-pound) chuck roast
- 1 green bell pepper, coarsely chopped
- 1 red bell pepper, coarsely chopped
- 1 very large onion, coarsely chopped
- 4 stalks celery, coarsely chopped
- 4 cloves garlic, minced
- ¹/2 cup beef broth
- 1 tablespoon dry mustard
- 1 tablespoon chili powder

- 1 cup honey hickory-smoked BBQ sauce or your favorite BBQ sauce

TEACHING NOTES

There is a large amount of pan juices that are left behind after removing meat from pot. Freeze for making a beef stew.

TEACHING NOTES

Great one-dish meal for family or for casual do ahead entertaining with a group of friends. All you need is a big green salad with some fresh fruit.

Mexican Cornbread Lasagna

SERVES 8

I originally used this recipe on a TV segment. It is a winning recipe from Lodge Manufacturing . . . the cast-iron people.

In a 10-inch, 5-quart cast-iron Dutch oven, brown beef, onions, and garlic. Drain. Add salsa and seasonings.

In a separate bowl, combine cottage cheese, Parmesan cheese, eggs, and chiles. Layer on top of meat mixture. Top with cheeses.

CORNBREAD: Combine cornbread ingredients except cheese. Pour over top of lasagna. Sprinkle with 4 ounces shredded Cheddar cheese. Bake at 375 degrees for 40 minutes or until cornbread is set and done.

1 1/2 pounds ground beef
2 cloves garlic, minced
2 cups chopped onions
1 (24-ounce) jar mild salsa
1 package taco seasoning
1 teaspoon cumin
1/2 teaspoon black pepper

16 ounces cottage cheese
1/3 cup Parmesan cheese
2 eggs
4 ounces canned mild green chiles

4 ounces Monterey Jack, shredded
4 ounces mozzarella cheese, shredded

CORNBREAD

1 cup self-rising cornmeal mix
2/3 cup sour cream
1/4 cup vegetable oil
4 ounces cream-style corn
1 egg
4 ounces canned mild green chiles

4 ounces shredded Cheddar cheese

Layered Tortilla Casserole

SERVES 8

TEACHING NOTES

Brown meat. Drain. Add onion and garlic and cook until soft. Add chili powder and cumin and stir to combine.

Add tomato sauce, green chiles, jalapeños, and salt. Simmer for 15 minutes.

While mixture simmers, heat 1 inch vegetable oil in iron skillet or pan of choice. Using tongs, dip tortillas into hot oil to soften. Do not brown. Drain on paper towels.

Whisk together cottage cheese and egg. Set aside.

TO ASSEMBLE: In a 9×13-inch casserole, place 1/3 meat mixture, followed by 1/2 the Monterey Jack cheese, 1/2 the cottage cheese mixture and 1/2 the tortillas. Repeat. End with meat mixture on top. Cover with grated Cheddar cheese. Bake for 30 minutes in preheated 350-degree oven or until hot and bubbly.

2 pounds ground chuck
1 onion, chopped
1 clove garlic, minced
2 tablespoons chili powder
1 teaspoon cumin

3 cups tomato sauce
1 (4-ounce) can chopped green chiles
2 tablespoons chopped pickled jalapeños (optional)
1 teaspoon salt

12 corn tortillas
vegetable oil

2 cups small-curd cottage cheese
1 egg, beaten

8 ounces Monterey Jack cheese
1 cup grated Cheddar cheese

89

TEACHING NOTES

- *This sounds like a lot of Chunky Red Sauce but it is a good basic staple to have on hand in the freezer. We used this sauce as the red sauce for lasagna and the marinara sauce for Parmesan Chicken.*

- *If you want to make the meatloaf but don't want to prepare the Chunky Red Sauce, you can use a thick marinara sauce. Reduce the amount to 1/2 cup.*

- *Meatloaf freezes well.*

- *If a substitution is necessary for the hot sauce, know how hot your sauce is and adjust amount accordingly, i.e., 1 tablespoon of Tabasco sauce would be too much!*

Spence's Meatloaf with Chunky Red Sauce
SERVES 6 TO 8

I take no credit for this recipe. John Spencer, Roosters on the Run's most competent cook, created this very popular ROTR offering.

Combine all ingredients and mix well. Fill 3 miniature loaf pans (5 1/4×3×2-inch) level to the top and pack down. Bake in preheated 350-degree oven for 50 to 60 minutes or to an internal temperature of 160 degrees.

- 2 1/2 pounds ground chuck
- 3/4 cup diced onion
- 1 1/2 cups panko (Japanese bread crumbs)
- 2 cloves garlic, minced
- 1/2 cup parsley, chopped
- 1 cup Chunky Red Sauce (below)
- 2 eggs
- 1 tablespoon Texas Pete hot sauce
- 1 tablespoon Montreal steak seasoning
- 1 teaspoon salt
- 1 teaspoon freshly ground black pepper

Chunky Red Sauce
MAKES 2 QUARTS

Sauté onions in olive oil until translucent. Add remaining ingredients and simmer one hour. Cool and store. Freezes well.

- 2 tablespoons olive oil
- 1 1/2 cups chopped onion

- 2 teaspoons minced garlic
- 1 (29-ounce) can tomato sauce
- 1 (29-ounce) can petite diced tomatoes
- 2 (14-ounce) jars pizza sauce
- 1 cup V-8 juice
- 1/2 cup fresh parsley, chopped
- 1 teaspoon dried oregano
- 1/2 teapoon dried thyme
- 1/4 cup fresh basil
- 3/4 cup water

Grilled Butterflied Leg of Lamb with Lemon Mint Aïoli

SERVES 8

Place lamb fat side down on cutting board. Cut into thick areas being careful not to cut all the way through. Fan the meat to create a uniform thickness. Insert metal skewers from side to side to bring the meat together and create a uniform thickness

In food processor fitted with a steel blade and with machine running, drop garlic through feed tube to mince. Remove lid, scrape down and add mint, orange and lemon zest and cumin. Process to purée. Add olive oil and process. Set aside.

Spread half of the mint mixture on cut side of lamb. Cover and refrigerate overnight.

Preheat grill. Place fat side down and sear. Watch for flare-ups. Turn and sear second side. Once seared, continue to cook by indirect heat or transfer to a 400-degree oven and cook to an internal temperature of 130 to 135 degrees for medium rare. Remove from heat source and spread with remaining mint mixture

Slice and serve at room temperature with Lemon Mint Aïoli.

LEMON MINT AÏOLI: In food processor fitted with a steel blade and with machine running, drop in garlic. Remove lid and add remaining ingredients. Season to taste with salt and pepper. Let stand at least 24 hours before using.

1 (3- to 4-pound) leg of lamb, boned

4 cloves garlic
1 cup fresh mint
zest of 2 oranges
1 tablespoon lemon zest
1 tablespoon cumin
6 tablespoons olive oil

LEMON MINT AÏOLI
1 large clove garlic

3/4 cup fresh mint, packed
1/2 cup mayonnaise
1/2 cup sour cream
zest of 2 lemons
3 tablespoons extra-virgin olive oil
1 tablespoon lemon juice
salt and freshly ground black pepper

TEACHING NOTES

- *Skewering the lamb not only creates a more uniform thickness but also will assist in the turning of the meat.*

- *Meats that need to cook for a longer period of time tend to become too charred on the grill. Counteract this by changing to indirect method of grilling, i.e., turn off one side of the gas grill and place meat over turned off area. Close lid and continue to cook. Alternatively, transfer to a sheet pan and finish in a 400-degree oven.*

- *This aïoli makes a phenomenal dipping sauce for chips or vegetables!*

- *When planting your garden, find a moist spot for a bed of mint, preferably Kentucky Colonel Spearmint. This larger leafed mint is the mint of choice for all my cooking, and also for mint juleps and mojitos.*

- *Did you know that you can identify plants in the mint family very quickly and easily? All plants in the mint family have square stems. Many of our most popular culinary herbs are part of this family . . . including basil, thyme, and oregano!*

91

TEACHING NOTES

- To French lamb racks, trim the rib bones of meat, fat, and gristle then scrape clean.

- Even with a cup of garlic cloves, garlic cream sauce is subtle and mellow. It is a wonderful do-ahead sauce for meats and even pasta.

Roasted Rack of Lamb with Garlic Cream Sauce SERVES A VARIABLE AMOUNT

GARLIC CREAM SAUCE: Peel garlic cloves. Cut in half and remove green sprout from center. In a small saucepan, cover garlic cloves with water. Bring to a simmer and cook for 15 to 20 minutes or until tender, adding just enough water to keep covered. Once garlic is tender, continue to cook until water is reduced to about a tablespoon. Add cream. Reduce to a sauce like consistency. Purée using an immersion blender, or blender, or food processor. Carefully correct consistency with more cream if necessary. Season with salt and pepper.

LAMB: Score the racks making shallow crisscross knife slashes in the sheath of fat. Combine garlic, mustard, olive oil, and salt. Brush mixture over meat. Combine panko, Parmesan cheese, and herbes de Provence. Press panko mixture onto lamb. Place lamb racks on roasting pan. Fold strip of foil over rib ends to prevent scorching.

Preheat oven to 425 degrees. Roast racks for 15 to 20 minutes or to an internal temperature of 125 degrees for rare or 130 degrees for medium. Cooking time will vary greatly depending on oven and size of lamb racks. Use a thermometer.

GARLIC CREAM SAUCE
1 cup garlic cloves
1 1/2 cups heavy cream
salt and freshly ground pepper

LAMB
2 racks of lamb, frenched

1 clove garlic, minced
3 tablespoons grainy mustard
3 tablespoons olive oil
1/2 teaspoon salt

1/2 cup panko (Japanese bread crumbs)
1/4 cup freshly grated Parmesan cheese
1 teaspoon herbes de Provence

Chinese Ribs

SERVES 6

If you ask my children what they want when they come home, this recipe is at the top of the list. It brings a smile to their faces and a twinkle to my eye! And it is a very easy recipe.

Sprinkle ribs with salt. Now cut butcher-prepared slabs into individual ribs. Set aside for 20 minutes.

In the wok, heat oil and sauté spareribs until lightly browned. Add soy sauce, sherry, ginger, garlic, and water. Cover. Simmer for 20 to 30 minutes, stirring occasionally. Remove cover and cook down until liquid begins to thicken.

Reduce heat to low, add bean sauce and brown sugar. Cook, uncovered, until ribs are completely glazed. Stir occasionally.

3 to 4 pounds baby back pork spareribs (have butcher cut slab of ribs in half lengthwise . . . perpendicular to the ribs . . . not into individual ribs)
1 1/2 teaspoons kosher salt
2 tablespoons oil

1/4 cup soy sauce
1/4 cup dry sherry
1/4 cup fresh ginger, minced
4 cloves garlic, minced
2 cups water

1 tablespoon sweet bean sauce
3 tablespoons brown sugar

TEACHING NOTES

- *Ribs can be done 1 to 2 days ahead and reheated, tightly covered, in oven or microwave. Recipe can be done without having ribs cut in half by butcher. They are just not as easy to manage when cooking or eating. Larger ribs will, of course, require longer cooking time while covered.*

- *A Cuisinart mini-chop makes mincing the ginger an easy task. It needs to be finely minced.*

- *Sweet bean sauce is available in Asian markets. It is usually in a small can. Once opened, it can be divided into portions and frozen. I have used hoisin sauce as a substitution and it works.*

93

TEACHING NOTES

- *Yes, cover the pans with plastic wrap and then foil. This ensures the tightness of the wrap and helps trap the steam.*

- *The meat is so tender, it falls off the bones. This is why it is important to refrigerate the ribs after cooking in the oven before grilling. Grill time is minimal . . . just long enough to mark the ribs and get them hot. Grilling can even be done ahead and then, before serving, reheat in the oven. It is next to impossible to overcook these ribs.*

- *Ribs freeze well.*

- *Change your dry rub and sauce for a different flavor profile each time. One of my favorites is to use Nantucket Off Shore Seasonings Dragon Rub then grill with World Art Foods Wasabi Plum Cooking Sauce. Think outside the box and come up with your own flavor combination.*

Grilled Baby Back Ribs   SERVES 8

Undoubtedly the easiest and best way to cook ribs. Amazingly, these ribs can be done totally ahead.

Rinse ribs and pat dry. Sprinkle 2 to 3 teaspoons of rub on both sides of each slab. Place a rack in a large roasting pan or sheet pan with sides. Place ribs on rack. Add as much water as possible to bottom of pan without it touching the rack. Cover with plastic wrap being careful to tuck edges of plastic wrap up under the edge of the pan. Then cover with extra wide heavy-duty aluminum foil carefully tucking foil to cover plastic wrap especially at edges.

Place in preheated 400-degree oven and bake for 3 hours. Remove from oven and uncover (watch out for the steam!). Refrigerate for several hours or overnight.

TO FINISH: Fire up the grill. Brush ribs with barbecue sauce. Spray ribs heavily with a vegetable oil spray. This will keep the ribs from sticking. Don't worry, it cooks away. Place this side down and grill, basting often, for 15 to 20 minutes or just until hot. Serve.

3 slabs baby back ribs
BBQ dry rub spice

barbecue sauce

94

Pork Loin with Apples, Prunes & Bourbon

SERVES 8

In a small saucepan, combine apples, 10 prunes, bourbon, and water. Heat over low heat for 3 or 4 minutes. Remove from heat. Set aside to use for sauce.

Butterfly pork loin. Using veal pounder, pound gently between 2 pieces of plastic wrap. Line up single row of prunes lengthwise down center of pork loin. Top with apple pieces, minced shallot, and thyme. Season with salt and pepper. Roll loin, beginning at long edge nearest you, and tie securely with butcher's twine.

Combine brown sugar and mustard. Carefully coat one side of the roast, saving any excess for later.

Heat oil in a heavy-bottomed ovenproof casserole. Place loin coated side down in hot pan. Brown thoroughly on this side, then spoon more brown sugar mixture on top. Carefully turn meat and brown this side. Repeat until all four sides are browned, 20 to 25 minutes. The sugar will caramelize; a little burning is okay and adds flavor . . . but watch carefully.

Warm 1/3 cup bourbon in microwave for 20 seconds. Pour over meat and flambé. When the flame is out, add the demi-glace, water, herbs, and any leftover brown sugar mixture. Bring to a simmer. Cover. Transfer to preheated 375-oven and cook for 1 hour.

Transfer meat to platter and keep warm. Transfer pan juices to small saucepan.

SAUCE: Drain cooled liquid from apples and prunes into a small bowl. Discard fruit. Stir in cornstarch. Add to pan juices. Bring to a simmer and cook gently until lightly thickened.

TO SERVE: Slice pork roast and serve with sauce.

2 Gala apples, medium dice
10 prunes
1/2 cup bourbon
1/4 cup water

4 pounds boneless pork loin
10 to 15 prunes
1 Gala apple, medium dice
1 shallot, minced
1 teaspoon thyme
salt and pepper

2/3 cup brown sugar, packed
1/2 cup Maille Dijon mustard
3 tablespoons grapeseed oil or
   vegetable oil

1/3 cup bourbon
1 tablespoon More than Gourmet
   Demi-Glace Gold
1 cup water
sprig of rosemary
large sprig of thyme

2 teaspooons cornstarch

Pork Tenders with Onion Marmalade, Mustard Cream Sauce & Raspberries

SERVES 6

Trim tenderloins of fat and silver skin. Place in Ziploc bag. Add marinade and rosemary branches. Marinate for 6 to 8 hours in the refrigerator.

Prepare charcoal grill or preheat gas grill. Add tenderloins and grill to internal temperature of 165 degrees.

ONION MARMALADE: In a large sauté pan, heat olive oil. Add onions and sauté until beginning to caramelize. Add raspberry vinegar, honey, and paprika. Reduce until thickened and glazed. Season to taste. Ten cups of onions yields about $3^1/2$ to 4 cups marmalade.

MUSTARD CREAM SAUCE:
In a 2-quart sauce pan or saucier, sauté shallots in olive oil until beginning to brown. Deglaze with white wine. Whisk in cream and mustard. Add thyme. Reduce to coating consistency. Can do ahead. Store in refrigerator.

TO SERVE: Slice pork into $1/2$-inch medallions. Place small mound of Onion Marmalade in center of plate. Surround with several pork medallions. Puddle Mustard Cream Sauce just in front of meat. Sprinkle with fresh raspberries.

2 pork tenderloins
**$1/4$ cup Dr. Pete's Burgundy Marinade
   or your favorite marinade**
2 (3-inch) pieces rosemary

ONION MARMALADE
$1/4$ cup olive oil
2 large onions (10 cups), sliced thin
$1/2$ cup raspberry vinegar
$1/3$ cup honey
1 teaspoon paprika
salt and freshly ground black pepper

MUSTARD CREAM SAUCE
3 tablespoons minced shallot
1 tablespoon olive oil
$1/2$ cup white wine
2 cups cream
$2^1/2$ tablespoons Dijon mustard
1 teaspoon dried thyme

fresh raspberries (garnish)

White Enchiladas

SERVES 6

Great way to use leftover cooked meats and a different twist on the usual tomato-based enchiladas.

Preheat oven to 350 degrees. Toss together meat of choice with chiles, corn, salsa, and salt.

Heat cream with garlic in a small sauté pan (big enough for tortilla just to fit). Set aside to cool.

TO ASSEMBLE: Dip each tortilla in cream. Remove, fill center of each tortilla with meat mixture. Roll and place seam side down in 2-quart casserole. Remove garlic from cream and pour remaining cream over tortillas. Top with grated cheese. Bake for 15 to 20 minutes or until warm and bubbly.

2 cups cooked chicken, pork, or shrimp, cubed, pulled or chopped
2 (4-ounce) cans chopped green chiles
1 (8-ounce) can corn, drained
1/4 or 1/2 cup salsa verde
1/2 teaspoon salt

2 cups heavy cream, warmed
2 cloves garlic, pressed
12 to 15 corn tortillas

8 ounces Monterey Jack cheese, grated
roasted red peppers, diced (optional garnish)

TEACHING NOTES

There are endless variations for this recipe. Even North Carolina BBQ can be used for meat. Want it spicy? Add jalapeños or simply use Monterey Jack cheese with jalapeños. A jar of roasted red peppers is a great condiment to keep on hand in the refrigerator, but if you don't have them you could use sliced green onions.

TEACHING NOTES

- *When you look at this recipe, it is overwhelming. But this is a great party for supper clubs and gourmet groups where the parts are divvied up. No one person has to do too much. Oh, and don't forget . . . put the guys on the grill. You can choose to do a variety of meats . . . beef, chicken, shrimp, or keep it simple with just one.*

- *Mojo Criollo marinades are available in traditional grocery stores but ethnic markets have a larger variety. I choose the one with the lowest sodium content. The Grilled Jumbo Shrimp (page 121) are also perfect for these fajitas. Use smaller shrimp.*

- *Styrofoam tortilla warmers for the microwave are available at ethnic markets. They are inexpensive and are the quickest, easiest way to heat flour tortillas.*

- *For Pulled Pork Fajitas, trim the fat from two 8-pound pork shoulders or butts. Place each piece of pork on a sheet of heavy-duty foil. Sprinkle each with 1 tablespoon kosher salt and seal the foil. Wrap each again with foil and place in a roasting pan. Bake at 275 degrees for 8 hours. Unwrap and pull the pork from the bones.*

A Fajita Buffet

SERVES A VARIABLE AMOUNT

Truly it is the parts that make the whole. Pull out the maracas. Put on the sombreros. Chill down the Corona. This is a party.

Choose a meat. Marinate beef or lamb overnight. Marinate chicken or shrimp for a few hours.

Peel onions, cut in half through the root. Slice into 1/4-inch slices. In fry pan or iron skillet, heat olive oil. Add onions and sauté until golden and caramelized. Add 3 to 4 tablespoons water to deglaze pan. Continue to cook until liquid is evaporated and onions are a rich brown color. Set aside for buffet.

Stem and seed peppers. Slice into 1/8- to 1/4-inch slices. In fry pan or iron skillet, heat olive oil. Add peppers and sauté until cooked through and are beginning to brown. Set aside for buffet.

TO SERVE: Platter meats on large colorful platter. Stack warm tortillas. Surround with bowls of Fresh Salsa, Guacamole, onions, peppers, cheese, and jalapeños. Don't forget the BBQ Sauce and White Sauce.

chicken, beef, lamb and/or shrimp
Mojo Criollo sauce/marinade

10 cups onions (at least)
3 to 4 tablespoons water
2 each green, red and yellow
bell peppers
olive oil

Fresh Salsa (page 25)
Guacamole (page 25)
Monterey Jack cheese, grated
pickled jalapeño slices

flour tortillas, warmed

BBQ Sauce for Fajitas (page 99)
White Sauce for Fajitas (page 99)

BBQ Sauce for Fajitas

MAKES 5 CUPS

This BBQ sauce is good on fajitas, quesadillas, and even ribs. It freezes well.

Combine all ingredients in a medium saucepan. Bring to a simmer and cook over low heat for 30 minutes, stirring frequently. Cool and serve.

1 1/2 cups canned diced tomatoes
1 1/2 cups ketchup
1 1/2 cups molasses
1/2 pound light brown sugar
4 ounces instant coffee
    (powder, do not reconstitute)
1/4 cup liquid smoke
1/4 cup **Worcestershire sauce**
2 tablespoons lemon juice

1 tablespoon chile powder
2 teaspoons ground cumin
1 1/2 teaspoons minced garlic
1 teaspoon ground mustard
1/2 teaspoon dried oregano
3/4 teaspoon freshly ground
    black pepper

White Sauce for Fajitas

MAKES 2 CUPS

Combine all ingredients. Whisk until blended and smooth. Refrigerate.

Add a spoonful of this sauce to your fajitas or quesadillas. It does not freeze.

1 cup mayonnaise
2/3 cup sour cream
1/2 cup milk
2 tablespoons lime juice
1 teaspoon white vinegar
1 1/2 teaspooons sugar

TEACHING NOTES

This is a great teaching recipe. The reduction sauce is the most basic of sauces and allows you to use your creativity and create your own flavor profile. Think about the flavor of the liquid used for reduction and then add a final ingredient that complements that flavor. Of course, herbs can be added to the flour that is used for dredging. For example, the following combinations would work well.

- *Curried Chicken and Bananas (add curry powder to flour or rub chicken with curry powder)*

- *Chicken with Basil & Sun-Dried Tomatoes (add fresh basil to sauce)*

- *Chicken with herbes de Provence & Black Olives (add herbes de Provence to flour for dredging and also to sauce)*

Variations, variations, variations . . . this is just food for thought. Create your own.

Chicken Breasts Many Ways

SERVES 6

This recipe was demonstrated over and over again to show that no matter what you have in your refrigerator, if you have a chicken breast, you've got a meal. I loved it when students would come back and tell me their "way" to dress up a chicken breast.

Place chicken breasts between two sheets of plastic wrap and using a flat-sided veal or meat pounder, pound to a thin and even thickness.

Combine flour, salt, and pepper. Dredge chicken in flour mixture. Shake off excess. In a sauté or fry pan, heat butter and olive oil until foam in butter begins to subside. Add chicken and brown on both sides. Remove from pan.

TO MAKE SAUCE: While pan is still hot, add either white wine, chicken stock, or brandy. Reduce until syrupy. Add cream and mustard. Reduce to desired sauce consistency. Add one of the final ingredients . . . choose chopped sun-dried tomatoes, or capers, or green peppercorns, or even bananas, or whatever you have found in your refrigerator and need to use.

6 boneless skinless chicken breasts

flour
salt
freshly ground black pepper

1 tablespoon butter
3 tablespoons olive oil

white wine or chicken stock or brandy
1 cup heavy cream
2 teaspoons Dijon mustard
sun-dried tomatoes or oil-cured olives or green peppercorns or bananas (whatever is in your refrigerator that you need to use)

Chicken Piccata

SERVES 4

This is one of the first recipes that I would teach a beginning cook.

Trim chicken breasts of any fat. Place between sheets of plastic wrap and using a veal pounder, pound to a thin, even thickness. Combine flour, salt, and pepper in flat dish. Dredge scallopine in flour mixture.

In a skillet, heat olive oil and butter until hot. Add scallopine and sauté until golden. Remove to a platter and keep warm.

Deglaze hot skillet by adding chicken stock or white wine. Add lemon juice and reduce pan juices to a glaze. Add capers and parsley. Remove from heat and whisk in butter. Adjust salt and pepper. Pour sauce over chicken and serve.

4 boneless skinless chicken breasts

1/3 cup flour
salt and freshly ground black pepper

3 tablespoons olive oil
1 tablespoon butter

1/2 cup chicken stock or white wine
juice of 1 lemon

3 tablespoons capers
1/4 cup parsley, minced
salt and freshly ground black pepper

2 or 3 tablespoons butter

Vinegar Chicken with Scallions

SERVES 4 TO 6

This was my Mother's recipe that she would use for large casual suppers. She was a woman who believed in doing things ahead with as little mess as possible!

Rinse chicken and pat dry. Sprinkle with sugar. Season with salt and pepper.

Heat sauté pan over medium heat. Add vegetable oil and butter. Increase heat to brown chicken, skin side down, until well browned. Turn and brown second side. Add vinegar and red pepper flakes. Cover. Transfer to preheated 350-degree oven and cook for 45 minutes. Remove from oven. Transfer chicken pieces to serving platter. Pour pan drippings into fat separator. Pour juices over chicken leaving fat in cup. (optional step: put pan juices without fat in saucepan and reduce to create a light glaze sauce.) Garnish with sliced scallions. Serve with rice.

1 whole chicken, cut up
3/4 teaspoon sugar
Maldon sea salt and freshly ground
    black pepper

2 tablespoons vegetable oil
3 tablespoons butter

1 cup cider vinegar
1 teaspoon red pepper flakes

scallions, sliced for garnish

TEACHING NOTES

Chicken Piccata

This is such a classic recipe and it teaches so much. Learn to trim, or even bone, a chicken breast. Learn to pound meat to make a scallopine. Learn to pan sear, and then deglaze a hot pan and make a quick sauce. Learn to develop your own recipe with your own flavor profile. For example, you can even change the meat to pork tenderloin by slicing the pork into 1/2-inch slices and pounding into a scallopine. Or spice up the flour mixture with cayenne.

A veal pounder is an essential piece of kitchen equipment. I particularly like a heavy, smooth surfaced pounder with an offset handle.

Vinegar Chicken with Scallions

- *Having your chicken patted very dry will help with browning and keep chicken from steaming. The very small amount of sugar also enhances browning. Browning this chicken to almost burning is what makes it so good. Don't be tempted to keep turning the chicken. Let it be and you will be rewarded!*

- *If making for a large group, browning will have to be done in batches. Follow recipe as directed, adding vinegar to each batch then transferring chicken to an electric roasting pan to complete cooking.*

TEACHING NOTES

- *To chiffonade an herb, stack the leaves, choosing the two largest leaves for the top and bottom of the stack. Roll up tightly like a cigar and slice into very thin slices. Once sliced, take knife and make 3 cuts across the slices. Voila! You have perfectly cut herbs. Basil bruises and turns black if it is chopped.*

- *To make roux, melt 1/2 cup butter in saucepan. Add 1/2 cup flour. Cook for 3 to 4 minutes, stirring constantly. Do not allow to brown. Transfer to storage container and refrigerate. Use as needed to thicken soups, sauces, etc.*

Chicken St. Andre

SERVES 8

Grilled chicken, spinach, fresh basil, and rice combine with a St. Andre cheese sauce to make a unique casserole.

Prepare the charcoal grill or preheat gas grill. Trim chicken breasts of fat. Sprinkle with balsamic rub. Place on grill and sear on both sides. Remove to sheet pan and place in preheated 400-degree oven to finish cooking. Depending on size of breasts, it should take 10 to 15 minutes. Remove and cool. When cool, pull meat into bite-size pieces.

SAUCE: In a 2-quart saucepan, combine half-and-half, water, balsamic rub, chicken base, and St. Andre cheese (cut in half with rind still attached). Bring to a simmer and cook until cheese is melted and rind is clean of cheese. Using tongs, remove rind. Add roux and continue to cook until thickened . . . about 5 to 10 minutes.

TOPPING: Combine all ingredients and set aside.

TO ASSEMBLE: In a large mixing bowl, toss together chicken, rice, spinach, and basil. Transfer to flat 3-quart baking dish. Evenly distribute sauce. Cover with topping.

Bake in preheated 350-degree oven for 30 minutes or until hot throughout.

4 boneless skinless chicken breasts
2 tablespoons Colorado Spice balsamic chicken rub

3 cups cooked basmati rice
1/2 pound baby spinach, coarsely chopped
I cup fresh basil, chiffonade

SAUCE
2 cups half-and-half
I cup water
I teaspoon Colorado Spice balsamic chicken rub
1 1/2 teaspoons Minor's chicken base
1/3 pound St. Andre cheese

3 tablespoons Roosters Roux (see Teaching Notes)

TOPPING
1/2 cup panko (Japanese bread crumbs)
1/4 cup freshly grated Parmesan cheese
2 teaspoons Italian seasoning
1/4 teaspoon salt
freshly ground black pepper

Fruit-Stuffed Chicken Breasts with Vinegar Sauce

SERVES 6 TO 8

This recipe is an adaptation of a recipe from Le Bec-Fin in Philadelphia. It was a perfect teaching recipe for our hands-on basic chicken classes. Don't let the length of the recipe scare you away.

Place chopped fruit in bowl. Cover with hot water and let stand until softened . . . about 15 minutes. Drain.

Heat olive oil in skillet. Add mushrooms and tomatoes. Sauté until all liquid is evaporated. Stir in fruit and cook for 2 or 3 minutes. Season with salt and freshly ground black pepper.

Cut pocket in chicken breast by making a horizontal slit through the thickest part of the breast. Open as to butterfly. Place a piece of spinach over bottom half of pocket. Top with fruit mixture. Close flap over filling and press gently to close.

Combine panko, Parmesan cheese, and Italian seasoning. In a flat dish, gently coat breasts with egg mixture then dip into bread crumbs. Be careful not to open pocket.

Heat olive oil in nonstick skillet and sauté breasts, placing in the pan on the side that would have been the skin. Turn and cook briefly. Transfer to baking sheet and place in preheated 350-degree oven until chicken is cooked through . . . about 15 to 20 minutes (depends on size of breast). Allow to rest for 5 minutes. Slice and serve with Vinegar Sauce.

VINEGAR SAUCE: Sauté shallots in olive oil until beginning to brown. Add sugar. Sauté until shallots are browned . . . stir constantly. Add vinegar. Bring to a boil. Cook for 2 or 3 minutes then add chicken and beef stock and reduce to 1 1/2 cups . . . about 20 to 25 minutes. Strain and serve over chicken.

1/2 cup dried apricots, chopped fine
1/4 cup dried cherries, chopped fine
2 tablespoons raisins, chopped fine

4 tablespoons olive oil
1 cup chopped portabello
    mushrooms
1 cup chopped seeded
    peeled tomatoes
salt and freshly ground black pepper

6 skinless boneless
    chicken breast halves

whole spinach leaves, uncooked

1 egg, beaten with 1/4 teaspoon salt
    and 1 tablespoon water

1 cup panko (Japanese
    bread crumbs)
1/4 cup freshly grated
    Parmesan cheese
1 teaspoon Italian seasoning

VINEGAR SAUCE
3/4 cup sliced shallots
1 tablespoon olive oil

1/4 cup sugar
1/4 cup cider vinegar
2 1/2 cups chicken stock
    (2 level teaspoons Minor's chicken
    base plus 2 1/2 cups water)
1 1/2 cups beef stock
    (1 level teaspoon Minor's beef
    base plus 1 1/2 cups water)

TEACHING NOTES

This recipe is easy to have done 99% ahead of time. Sauce can be done ahead. Chicken can be completed to the point of transferring to oven.

Once you have mastered stuffing the breasts and breading them, think about other stuffing combinations and flavor profiles . . . sauté fennel, leeks, and eggplant that have been minced, add roasted red peppers. Cool. Stuff into breast with a few feta cheese crumbles. That is your Mediterranean profile, now you come up with an Asian profile. See how it works.

103

TEACHING NOTES

- *Always make extra of these to keep on hand in the freezer. Freeze individually then wrap each in plastic wrap and store in plastic bag in freezer.*

- *Thai fish sauce has a horrific (yes, horrific) smell but it does not taste the way it smells. Use it!*

Thai Chicken Cakes with Rice Wine Chile Sauce

SERVES 6 TO 8

This is a favorite dinner served with Asian Spiced Slaw (page 54). It was a favorite combo for Roosters on the Run customers.

Trim chicken breasts of fat and tendon. Cut into chunks and place in the food processor fitted with the steel blade. Pulse on and off until chicken is minced. Do not purée. Transfer to mixing bowl.

Add remaining ingredients. Stir to combine. Using wet hands, shape into cakes about 3 to 4 inches in diameter.

In a nonstick skillet, heat vegetable oil. Add chicken cakes and sauté until golden and cooked through . . . about 10 to 12 minutes. Serve drizzled with Rice Wine Chile Sauce.

RICE WINE CHILE SAUCE:
Combine all the ingredients. Mix well.

2 pounds boneless skinless
   chicken breasts

4 medium shallots, minced
1 1/2 tablespoons Thai fish sauce
1 tablespoon minced cilantro
1/4 cup canned coconut milk
1 teaspoon curry powder
1 teaspoon sugar
1/2 teaspoon salt
1/4 teaspoon red pepper flakes

3 to 4 tablespoons vegetable oil

RICE WINE CHILE SAUCE
1/4 cup Asian sweet chili sauce
1 tablespoon rice wine vinegar

Egg Fu Yung

TEACHING NOTES

*This is perfect for Sunday night supper.
And it is so very quick and easy!*

Combine meat with bamboo shoots, onions, celery, and bean sprouts. Beat eggs with salt. Pour over meat and vegetables.

In a nonstick fry pan, heat enough oil to cover bottom of pan. Ladle egg/vegetable mixture into hot skillet . . . pancake size. Cook until set on first side, turn and finish on second side. Continue until all mixture is used. Serve hot, topped with sauce and garnished with green onion slices and sesame seeds.

SAUCE: In a small saucepan, combine all ingredients. Bring to a boil, stirring constantly. Cook until thickened. Add final tablespoon of cream sherry just before serving. Serve hot.

1/2 cup cooked meat (chicken, pork, shrimp, beef)
1/2 cup bamboo shoots, julienned
1/2 cup chopped onions
1/2 cup chopped celery
1 cup fresh bean sprouts

3 eggs
1 teaspoon salt

vegetable oil

green onions, sliced
sesame seeds, toasted

SAUCE
1 1/2 cups chicken broth
2 tablespoons cornstarch
1 tablespoon soy sauce
1 tablespoon cream sherry
1 teaspoon sugar

1 tablespoon cream sherry

TEACHING NOTES

Alternatives to Basil Pesto

- *Bella Cucina Sun-dried Tomato Pesto and add 2 or 3 teaspoons smoked paprika for a smoky sauce*

- *Deglaze with brandy and increase mustard to 1 tablespoon for a brandy sauce*

- *Sauté coarsely chopped shiitake mushrooms in pan juices, deglaze with sherry, add cream and a touch of mustard and reduce to desired consistency for a mushroom sauce*

Having skin-on chicken breasts is important to this recipe. Skin should be thoroughly browned and crisp before turning so don't be in a hurry to turn the chicken. It should be very brown on the first side . . . more than half done. Honestly, it is an excellent dish when it comes from the oven without any sauce . . . just the pan juices.

Pan-Seared Chicken Breasts

SERVES 6 TO 8

Choose your flavor profile for a different dish every time! This recipe was always a part of our basic chicken class. Boning a chicken breast is really very simple.

Bone chicken breasts, keeping skin intact. Season with salt and pepper. Preheat 12- or 14-inch sauté pan. Add olive oil and butter. Place chicken, skin side down, in hot pan. Sauté until deep golden. Turn and transfer to oven for 5 to 10 minutes (depends on size of breast and how long it was cooked on top of stove).

Remove pan from oven. Transfer chicken to platter and cover to keep warm. Heat pan on top of stove. Deglaze with white wine. Add mustard, cream, and pesto. Reduce to a light coating consistency. Pour juices that have accumulated on platter into sauce

TO SERVE: Slice each breast diagonally into 3 pieces. Top with sauce.

6 chicken breasts, bone-in with skin
salt and freshly ground black pepper

2 tablespoons olive oil
1 tablespoon butter

1/4 to 1/2 cup white wine
2 teaspoons Dijon mustard
1 cup heavy cream
2 or 3 tablespoons classic basil pesto

Cajun Tasso & Noodles

SERVES 8

I make no apologies for the canned soup . . . the ease of preparation and the other ingredients make up for it!

Choose method for cooking chicken:

METHOD 1 (PREFERRED): Place bone-in chicken breasts in Cameron Stovetop Smoker. Slide lid in place and smoke with 2 tablespoons hickory chips for 30 minutes. Uncover, allow to cool and tear into bite-size pieces.

METHOD 2: If smoking is not an option for you, rub the chicken breasts with olive oil and a creole spice. Prepare the charcoal grill or preheat the gas grill. Grill chicken until done. Cool and pull into bite-size pieces.

Combine sauce ingredients and set aside.

Line 9×13-inch flat casserole with cooked fettuccine. Top with chicken and tasso, then sauce. Sprinkle with cheese and green onions. Bake in preheated 350-degree oven for 30 to 35 minutes or until bubbly.

4 skinless bone-in chicken breasts
1 (8-ounce) package fettuccine, cooked
6 ounces Cajun tasso, diced

SAUCE
1 can cream of mushroom soup
8 ounces sour cream
1 cup mayonnaise
1 1/2 tablespoons Dijon mustard
1/4 cup dry sherry

TOPPING
8 ounces sharp Cheddar cheese, grated
1 small bunch green onions, sliced

MEAT · POULTRY · SEAFOOD

TEACHING NOTES

- *The very easy to use stovetop smoker works extremely well for cooking without fat while adding lots of flavor. Meats are extremely tender and juicy because you are actually steaming.*

- *Shrimp can be substituted for chicken.*

107

TEACHING NOTES

- *Thigh meat is essential to this recipe and is popular even with people who say they don't eat dark meat. I like to serve this dish in flat soup bowls with black Italian Venere rice or a black Thai rice or wild rice (in that order) in the center and the chicken banked up against the rice. Garnish with orange sections and a drizzle of pan juices.*

- *For best results, make sure chicken is well pan-seared . . . almost crusty.*

Provençal Chicken with Oranges & Black Olives

SERVES 4

A beautiful center of the plate presentation.

Rinse chicken and pat dry. Coat evenly with cumin. Season with salt and pepper.

Heat nonstick sauté pan or wok over medium heat. Add olive oil to cover bottom of pan. Add chicken, skin side down, and cook until well browned. Turn and cook briefly on second side. Chicken should not be done at this point. Remove from pan.

Drain all but a small amount of fat from pan. Add onions and garlic. Sauté briefly. Add juices, stock, and cumin. Bring to a simmer. Return chicken to pan. Add olives. Cover and simmer for 25 minutes or until chicken is cooked through.

Serve garnished with orange sections.

6 to 8 boneless skinless
  chicken thighs
2 tablespoons ground cumin
salt and freshly ground black pepper
olive oil

1 cup chopped onion
1 heaping tablespoon minced garlic

1/4 cup orange juice
2 tablespoons lemon juice
1/2 cup chicken stock
3/4 teaspoon cumin
3/4 cup oil-cured black olives, pitted

3 oranges, peeled and sectioned

Chicken Marbella

SERVES 8

Even those who say they don't eat dark meat love it.

In a large bowl, combine garlic, oregano, salt, pepper, vinegar, and olive oil. Stir to combine. Add prunes, figs, olives, capers, and bay leaves. Pour over chicken. Seal in a Ziploc bag and marinate overnight in the refrigerator.

Preheat oven to 350 degrees. Arrange chicken in single layer in a shallow baking/roasting pan. Add marinade, spreading evenly. Sprinkle with brown sugar and pour white wine around chicken.

Bake for 1 hour.

Transfer chicken to serving platter. Spoon prunes, figs, olives, capers and some pan juices over. Sprinkle with parsley and serve.

4 large cloves garlic, minced
3 tablespoons dried oregano
coarse salt and pepper
1/3 cup red wine vinegar
1/3 cup olive oil

1 cup prunes, pitted, cut in half
1 cup dried figs, stemmed, cut in half
1/2 cup pitted Spanish olives or
    pitted picholines
1/2 cup capers
4 bay leaves

16 to 20 boneless skinless
    chicken thighs

1/2 cup brown sugar
3/4 cup white wine

fresh parsley, minced (garnish)

TEACHING NOTES

Chicken Marbella

- *Dark meat is important because it doesn't dry out. I love using the thighs because they are inexpensive, can be used boneless and skinless (thus less fat), and are fall-apart tender after they are cooked.*

Do-Ahead Crowd-Pleasing Menu

- *Chicken Marbella (left)*

- *Steamed Brown Rice*

- *Crunchy Romaine and Parmesan with Lemon Juice Vinaigrette (page 58)*

- *Focaccia (page 41)*

- *Fresh Apple Walnut Cake with Brown Sugar Glaze (page 135)*

109

TEACHING NOTES

Sometimes baguettes are just too thick for a sandwich. So for a thinner baguette, cut baguette in half lengthwise then cut off another slice each side of the first cut. You have just removed the center of the bread and no one will ever know.

Grilled Sausages with Onions & Peppers

SERVES 4

Perfect for last minute patio entertaining or a quick family supper. Specialty sausages have become very popular. Usually lower in fat, these sausages are also an upscale alternative to the hot dog!

Place sausages in fry pan in ¹/4-inch water. Cover, bring to a simmer and cook for 5 to 10 minutes. Remove lid, increase heat to high and continue to cook to evaporate liquid. At this point, you can continue to cook in fry pan until golden or transfer to outdoor grill to finish.

Meanwhile, heat olive oil in sauté pan. Add peppers and onions and cook until tender and begin to brown and caramelize. This will do best if just left alone and stirred only occasionally.

Cut baguette into 4 sections. Split each section in half horizontally and toast in oven or on grill.

TO SERVE: Spread baguette with mustard of choice. Top with sausage, and then peppers and onion.

4 chicken or turkey sausages, or
   other specialty sausage

1 tablespoon olive oil
2 red bell peppers, cut into strips
1 yellow bell pepper, cut into strips
1 large onion, sliced thin

1 French or sourdough baguette
mustard of choice

Polenta, Sausage, & Portabello Casserole

SERVES 6 TO 8

Combine milk, butter, and salt in a heavy saucepan and heat to a simmer. Slowly add the polenta in a thin stream . . . whisking constantly. Lower heat and continue stirring until mixture has thickened and leaves the sides of the pan . . . about 20 minutes. Stir in cheeses. Pour into a greased 3-quart casserole. Set aside.

Cut sausage into 3/4-inch pieces. In a medium fry pan, sauté until lightly browned and cooked through. Remove. Cut mushrooms into 1-inch pieces and sauté until tender and juices have evaporated.

TO ASSEMBLE: Top polenta with cooked sausage, and then mushrooms. Spread evenly with Chunky Red Sauce followed by Parmesan cheese. Finish with mozzarella cheese.

Bake in preheated 375-degree oven for 30 minutes or until bubbly. Let stand for 10 minutes before serving

Freezes well.

3 1/2 to 4 cups milk
1 tablespoon butter
1/2 teaspoon salt
1 cup polenta

1/4 cup Parmesan cheese, grated
1/2 cup Comté or Gruyère cheese, grated

12 ounces chicken and pesto sausage

1 1/2 cups Chunky Red Sauce (page 90) or your favorite jarred pasta sauce
8 ounces portabello mushrooms
1/2 cup grated Parmesan cheese

8 ounces mozzarella cheese, grated

TEACHING NOTES

- *Polenta can be cooked in double boiler and only has to be stirred a couple of times. It takes at least an hour. Grits and oatmeal also work in a double boiler.*

- *Using milk or half-and-half to cook polenta and grits yields a much richer product. Even skim milk is better than water.*

111

TEACHING NOTES

The debate rages between fresh vs. frozen turkeys. It is my experience that there is not a great difference. The secret is not to overcook the turkey.

Many students found it unorthodox to add hard-boiled eggs to the turkey gravy. It is not Thanksgiving to me without the eggs in the gravy!

If you like the giblets, you can cook them in the turkey roasting pan during the last half hour of cooking time . . . chop them up and add them to the gravy.

I taught this Southern Thanksgiving class 3 or 4 times every October/ November. By the time the real Thanksgiving came around I wanted a steak!

Roast Turkey with Pan Gravy

SERVES 8

TURKEY: Preheat oven to 325 degrees. Remove neck and giblets. Rinse turkey inside and out, pat dry. Fold neck skin under body and secure with skewer if desired. Tie drumsticks together with kitchen twine and tuck wings under back. Rub outside of turkey with butter. Season inside and out with poultry seasoning, salt, and pepper. Place turkey on rack set in large deep roasting pan. Add 1 to 2 cups water to bottom of pan. You want at least $1/2$- to 1-inch water in bottom of pan. Place in preheated oven. After the first hour, baste every 20 to 30 minutes with pan juices. A 12- to 14-pound turkey will cook in about 3 hours. Pay close attention to "bird watcher thermometer" (they really do work). But also, to check for doneness insert instant read thermometer into thickest part of thigh. The internal temperature should be 170 to 180 degrees.

GRAVY: Drain pan drippings into a fat separator or skim fat from pan drippings. Do not discard fat. Pour de-fatted pan drippings into a measuring cup. Add chicken stock to make a total of 4 cups.

Transfer reserved fat to 2-quart saucepan and heat until bubbling. Add flour . . . additional butter may be needed if there is not enough fat on the drippings. You need about $1/4$ cup fat. Cook for 1 to 2 minutes. Add pan drippings/chicken stock mixture and cook until thickened.

Just before serving, add hard-boiled eggs and cook until hot.

TURKEY
1 (12- to 14-pound) fresh turkey
butter
poultry seasoning
salt and freshly ground black pepper

GRAVY
pan drippings
2 to 3 cups chicken stock

5 tablespoons flour

8 hard-boiled eggs, sliced

Pan-Seared Duck Breast with Sarsaparilla Sauce

SERVES 8

MEAT · POULTRY · SEAFOOD

Preheat oven to 400 degrees.

SAUCE: Combine 3/4 cup sarsaparilla and orange juice. Reduce to a light syrup. Skim if necessary to remove solids that float to the top. Add glace de canard, water, and 1/2 cup more sarsaparilla. Reduce by one third. Combine arrowroot and water. Just before serving, add arrowroot mixture to reduction and simmer just until thickened.

DUCK: Make 3 or 4 slashes diagonally through skin and fat. Sprinkle with kosher salt. Preheat skillet until hot. Place duck breasts skin side down in hot skillet. Sear for 5 to 7 minutes on first side before turning. Fat should be rendered and skin crisp. Turn and transfer to preheated oven for 5 minutes or so . . . depends on the size of the duck breast. Meat should be slightly resistant to the touch . . . as it would be for a medium steak.

TO SERVE: Allow duck to rest for at least 5 minutes then cut each on the diagonal into 3 slices. Fan and top with sauce.

DUCK
8 boneless duck breasts
kosher salt

SAUCE
3/4 cup sarsaparilla soda (root beer)
I cup freshly squeezed orange juice
1/2 package (I tablespoon) More
   Than Gourmet glace de canard

I 1/2 cups water
1/2 cup sarsaparilla soda

I teaspoon arrowroot
I teaspoon water

TEACHING NOTES

This is my choice for my birthday dinner. Unfortunately, I usually have to cook it!

- *Pan-Seared Duck Breast with Sarsaparilla Sauce (left)*

- *Corn Flan (page 66)*

- *Orange-Glazed Salt-Roasted Beets (page 65)*

- *Chocolate Decadence with Fresh Raspberries (page 148)*

TEACHING NOTES

- *This recipe can be done days ahead to the point of reheating in the oven. If you want to do a large amount, use an electric roaster and cook on 250 degrees until meat is tender. It will not take 10 hours.*

- *Don't throw away the fat that is rendered during the cooking. Drain and strain it. Refrigerate or freeze and use for sautéing potatoes.*

- *Meat can be pulled from duck legs and used for quesadillas with a mild BBQ sauce and cheese (Comté, goat, etc). Or put on a small roll or cornbread muffin with some orange marmalade or hot mustard for an appetizer.*

Duck Leg Confit

SERVES 12

Traditionally, confit is cooked in large amounts of fat and then the meat is stored and preserved in this fat out of refrigeration. So, my French counterparts would say this is not actually a confit since it is not cooked in this manner. But, the same slow-cooking process works well and the results are deliciously tender.

RUB: In a mini processor or with a mortar and pestle, crush all ingredients except onions. Liberally sprinkle on both sides of the duck legs. Refrigerate for at least 12 hours. Remove and rinse. Pat dry with a clean towel.

Place a layer of onions in the bottom of a large Crock Pot. Add half the duck legs. Add another layer of onions and then the remaining duck legs. Finish with a layer of onions. Cook on low for 10 hours. Carefully lift duck legs from fat. If using right away, proceed to oven transfer. If storing, place on sheet pan and refrigerate then package.

TO SERVE: Preheat oven to 400 degrees, preferably convection. Place duck legs on jelly roll pan. Bake until heated through . . . 15 to 20 minutes. Serve with lentils and sautéed apples.

---

12 duck legs with thighs

RUB
3 juniper berries
2 bay leaves
4 garlic cloves
2 tablespoons chopped
   fresh rosemary
3 tablespoons dried thyme
1 tablespoon salt
1 tablespoon freshly ground
   black pepper

6 to 8 cups onions, coarsely chopped

114

Asian Steamed Fish Fillets   SERVES 6

Stack fish fillets in two separate stacks, creating an even brick shape.

Combine marinade ingredients. Pour over fish fillets and marinate for at least 30 minutes.

Place in steamer or use a bamboo steamer. Spoon some marinade over fillets. Cover and steam over boiling water for 10 to 12 minutes (depends on thickness of fish).

Garnish with a sprinkle of green onions and cilantro.

6 flounder or scrod or other flat white fish fillets

MARINADE
1/2 cup thinly sliced green onions
1/4 cup soy sauce
2 tablespoons rice wine vinegar
1 1/2-inch piece fresh ginger, peeled, thinly julienned
2 tablespoons oriental sesame oil
2 teaspoons sugar
2 cloves garlic, minced
1/4 teaspoon red pepper flakes

1/4 to 1/2 cup sliced green onions (garnish)
2 or 3 tablespoons chopped cilantro (garnish)

Grilled Grouper with Herbed Kumquat Butter   SERVES 6

Combine marinade ingredients in Ziploc bag. Add grouper and marinate for at least 30 minutes and up to one hour. Prepare charcoal or preheat gas grill. Place fish on prepared grill and cook for 5 or 6 minutes per side. Timing depends on thickness of fish and temperature of fire. Remove and immediately top with Kumquat Butter.

KUMQUAT BUTTER: In food processor fitted with a steel blade and with motor running, drop in garlic. Add kumquats and pulse to chop. Remove lid, scrape down sides and add remaining ingredients. Process until smooth. Remove from food processor. Place on square of plastic wrap and shape into roll. Refrigerate or freeze until ready to use.

6 grouper fillets

MARINADE
1/4 cup olive oil
3 tablespoons red wine vinegar
zest and juice of 1 orange
salt and freshly ground black pepper

KUMQUAT BUTTER
1 clove garlic
3 preserved kumquats, drained and seeds removed
1 cup butter, cut in pieces
2 or 3 tablespoons syrup from kumquats
3 tablespoons fresh parsley
2 tablespoons fresh basil
1/2 teaspoon salt
freshly ground black pepper

MEAT · POULTRY · SEAFOOD

TEACHING NOTES

Asian Steamed Fish Fillets

Measure the thickness of the fish. It takes 10 to 12 minutes to cook each inch of fish.

Grilled Grouper with Herbed Kumquat Butter

- *The number one complaint I heard in cooking school about grilling fish was "my fish always sticks." Here are a few pointers to help you out. First, clean grill rack well with wire brush. Second, spray the fish fillet (not the grill) with a heavy coating of vegetable oil spray (don't worry, it cooks off quickly). And third, make sure the grill is very hot before placing fish on it. And finally, do not try to turn it too soon.*

- *Preserved kumquats are a jarred product that is found in specialty food stores.*

115

TEACHING NOTES

- *I am a huge proponent of the electric steamer. It is an easy way to cook vegetables and fish and oh so healthy.*

- *Grapeseed oil is called for in the recipe because of its high smoke point. It really does a very good job of finishing the dish with a sizzle. Peanut oil could be substituted.*

Sizzling Fish Fillets with Green Onions & Ginger

SERVES 4

It's quick, it's easy, and the Asian flavor profile is a real winner.

Stack fish fillets one on top of the other to make a brick of even thickness. Place in electric steamer or bamboo steamer. Top with an even layer of ginger, and then onions. Cover and steam until done. Once water comes to a simmer, allow 10 to 12 minutes per inch of thickness. Fish is done when it has lost its translucence and is opaque throughout.

Remove from steamer to heatproof platter. Drizzle with soy sauce. Heat grapeseed oil until it is beginning to smoke. Pour hot oil over fish.

TO SERVE: Slice fish into 4 portions and place on plates. Drizzle with juices from platter.

2 or 3 haddock or flounder fillets

3 tablespoons finely minced fresh ginger

1/2 cup green onions, small slice

3 tablespoons soy sauce

1/4 cup grapeseed oil

Salmon with Soy & Onions

Ladies Home Journal *featured this recipe in their February 1994 issue. It was part of an article "No Fail Recipes from the Pros." To quote the magazine . . . "This simple salmon dish is an old favorite of cooking teacher Mary James Lawrence. She teaches it to inspire confidence about preparing fish."*

In a 3-quart sauté pan or skillet with lid, heat olive oil over medium high heat; add onions and cook, stirring occasionally, until translucent . . . about 5 minutes.

Place salmon fillets on what would have been the skin side down over onions in skillet. Pour on soy sauce. Cover and simmer over medium low heat until salmon is just opaque in center . . . 10 to 12 minutes. Transfer salmon to platter. Cover to keep warm.

Increase heat, and continue cooking onions and soy sauce until slightly thickened . . . 2 to 3 minutes. Pour over salmon and serve.

2 tablespoons olive oil

2 cups coarsely chopped onions

4 salmon fillets (6 ounces each), skinned

1/2 cup reduced-salt soy sauce

MEAT · POULTRY · SEAFOOD

TEACHING NOTES

Serve this simple dish with steamed or roasted asparagus and orzo seasoned with olive oil, thyme, salt, and pepper. Simplicity is the key.

TEACHING NOTES

Seared Sea Bass with Red Wine Balsamic Beurre Blanc

- *The amount of olive oil for pan sautéeing fish depends on the size pan you are using. There should be just enough to cover the bottom of the pan. Finishing seared items in the oven allows you to turn your attention to the sauce.*

- *When making the sauce, move the pan on and off the heat so that the butter does not melt too fast. This will prevent the sauce from separating.*

- *Wine and vinegars for sauce can be reduced early in the day then reheated just before service, adding butter at that time.*

- *Menu suggestions: Serve banked against seared greens (Swiss chard, kale, spinach, etc.) with a few roasted potatoes to the side.*

Seared Sea Bass with Red Wine Balsamic Beurre Blanc

SERVES 6

Season flour with salt and freshly ground black pepper. Dredge sea bass in flour mixture. In a nonstick fry pan over medium high heat, heat olive oil and butter just until butter begins to stop bubbling. Place fillets skin side up in the hot pan. Sear for 2 or 3 minutes. Turn and transfer to 400-degree oven to complete cooking . . . 5 to 8 minutes depending on thickness of fish. Fish is done when it is opaque throughout.

SAUCE: In a medium nonreactive saucepan, combine wine and vinegars. Reduce until syrupy. On and off the heat, whisk in pieces of cold butter.

flour
salt and pepper
6 (6-ounce) portions sea bass, skinned

3 to 4 tablespoons olive oil
1 tablespoon butter

SAUCE
1 cup red wine
3/4 cup balsamic vinegar
1/4 cup rice wine vinegar

1/2 cup cold butter, cut into 8 pieces

Tilapia with Brown Butter & Caper "Flowers"

SERVES 8

Combine flour, Old Bay, salt, and pepper. Dredge fish in flour mixture. Heat olive oil and butter in sauté pan. Sauté fillets until golden. Set aside and keep warm.

BROWN BUTTER & CAPER SAUCE: In a small saucepan, heat grapeseed oil until smoking hot. Add capers and cook until they pop open like flowers. Drain on paper towels.

In a small skillet, melt butter and cook over medium heat until it becomes a nutty brown. Add vinegar. Whisk. Add caper "flowers." Serve over fish.

1 cup flour
1 tablespooon Old Bay seasoning
1 teaspoon salt
freshly ground black pepper

8 tilapia fillets or other flat fish fillets

3 tablespoons olive oil
1 tablespoon butter

BROWN BUTTER & CAPER SAUCE
1/3 cup grapeseed oil or peanut oil
1/3 cup capers
6 tablespoons butter
2 tablespoons sherry vinegar

Southwestern Crab Cakes

MAKES 40 (3/4-OUNCE) COCKTAIL SIZE CRAB CAKES OR 5 OR 6 ENTRÉE-SIZE

Gently pick crabmeat for cartilage. Toss with tomato. Add bread crumbs with dry spices. In a separate bowl, combine egg, salsa, cilantro, mayonnaise, and mole sauce. Add to crabmeat mixture and gently combine.

TO SHAPE INTO CRAB CAKES:
For cocktail size cakes, use a #60 ice cream scoop (about 2 teaspoons of mixture each) and place mounds of crabmeat mixture onto a piece of foil or parchment. Using your fingertips, twirl each mound into round shape with straight sides. Pat gently on top and place on sheet pan until all are shaped and ready to fry.

TO COOK: Heat 1/4 inch of oil in nonstick skillet. Add crab cakes and sauté until golden. Turn and finish. Drain on paper towels. Can be done ahead and reheated in 350-degree oven. Crab cakes freeze well.

Serve with a dot of sauce on top.

SAUCE: Combine all sauce ingredients. Let stand for at least 1 hour before serving.

CAKES
- 1 pound backfin or claw crabmeat
- 1/2 cup seeded and finely diced Roma tomatoes

- 1 cup panko (Japanese bread crumbs)
- 1 1/2 teaspoons salt
- 1 teaspoon chili powder
- 1/2 teaspoon ground cumin
- 1 1/2 tablespoons minced shallot
- 1 teaspoon minced garlic

- 1 egg
- 1/2 cup salsa
- 1 tablespoon chopped cilantro
- 1 tablespoon mayonnaise
- 1 teaspoon mole sauce

vegetable oil or grapeseed oil

SAUCE
- 3/4 cup mayonnaise
- 1/4 cup sour cream
- 2 teaspoons lime juice
- 1 teaspoon chile powder
- 1/2 teaspoon mole sauce or to taste

119

Scalloped Oysters

- *Everyone should be at the table and ready to be served when you bring the oysters out of the oven. They are like a soufflé and begin to fall almost immediately, but still so delicious.*

- *You can layer the oysters and crackers early in the day. Add half-and-half just before baking.*

- *No salt necessary for this dish because of the saltine crackers.*

Scalloped Oysters

SERVES 8 TO 10 AS PART OF A THANKSGIVING BUFFET

Heavily butter a 2-quart gratin or flat casserole. Scatter a few very coarsely broken crackers in bottom of dish. Top with a few oysters. Continue to layer until all crackers and oysters are used. When pan is half full, dot with 3 tablespoons of the butter and season with freshly ground black pepper. Add half-and-half to just the top of the crackers. Dot with the remaining butter and season again with freshly ground black pepper.

Bake in preheated 400-degree oven for 25 to 30 minutes or until puffed and golden. Serve immediately.

2 (8-ounce) cans fresh oysters
    with liquor

8 to 10 ounces (2 sleeves or more)
    Zesta saltine crackers
freshly ground black pepper
1/2 cup butter
half-and-half

Pan-Seared Sea Scallops   SERVES 4

Pat scallops dry. Combine orange zest, orange juice, olive oil, and cinnamon in Ziploc bag. Add scallops and marinate for 15 to 20 minutes. Drain. Dredge in small amount of flour seasoned with salt and pepper.

Preheat empty sauté pan until hot. Add olive oil just to cover the bottom of the pan. Add scallops. Do not crowd the pan. Sear on first side until brown . . . about 1 to 2 minutes. Turn and continue to cook for 1 to 2 more minutes. Add orange juice. Juice should evaporate quickly. Season with salt and pepper. Remove and serve.

12 sea scallops
zest of 1/2 orange
2 tablespoons fresh orange juice
1 tablespoon olive oil
1/4 teaspoon cinnamon

flour
salt and freshly ground black pepper

olive oil
juice of 1 orange
salt and freshly ground black pepper

Grilled Jumbo Shrimp

Serve alone or with salads, pastas, or risottos.

In a bowl, combine garlic, lemon zest and juice, olive oil, oregano, red pepper flakes, salt, and pepper. Place in Ziploc bag with shrimp and marinate in refrigerator for 1 hour.

Prepare charcoal grill or preheat gas grill. Remove shrimp from marinade. Thread onto skewers, going through the tip and tail to keep shrimp from spinning when turning. Cook for about 3 or 4 minutes per side . . . it totally depends on size of shrimp and temperature of fire.

2 or 3 tablespoons minced garlic
zest of 1 lemon
3 tablespoons fresh lemon juice
1/2 cup extra-virgin olive oil
2 tablespoons dried oregano
1/4 teaspoon red pepper flakes
1/2 teaspoon salt
freshly ground black pepper

2 pounds jumbo shrimp, peeled and deveined

Shrimp Roll with Caper Sauce

SERVES 4 TO 6

In a small bowl, combine mayonnaise, shallots, capers, mustard, Worcestershire sauce, tarragon, and hot sauce. Add to shrimp

Cut baguette into desired sandwich size sections. Split for a sandwich without cutting all the way through. Place on baking sheet and heat for 5 to 8 minutes in preheated 350-degree oven

Open baguette pieces and top with shrimp mixture. Serve.

1/4 cup mayonnaise
1 tablespoon minced shallots
2 teaspoons capers, drained
1 teaspoon Dijon mustard
1/2 teaspoon Worcestershire sauce
1/4 teaspoon dried tarragon
1/4 teaspoon Texas Pete hot sauce or to taste

4 cups cooked shrimp
(about 1 1/2 pounds packaged precooked shrimp)

French baguettes

MEAT · POULTRY · SEAFOOD

TEACHING NOTES

Grilled Jumbo Shrimp

I used this recipe to teach how not to overcook shrimp. Since shrimp come in many sizes, it is difficult to give an exact cooking time. Therefore, my advice to the wary cook is to watch closely. Shrimp should be firm to touch when done but if you see it begin to shrink in size, you have overcooked it.

Shrimp Roll with Caper Sauce

- *This is a very quick meal to prepare when you buy precooked shrimp. Just remember to pat them very dry before mixing with sauce.*

- *Sauce is excellent as a dipping sauce for shrimp or vegetables.*

TEACHING NOTES

- *Grits can be cooked in a double boiler. It takes much longer . . . as much as 1 to 1 1/2 hours . . . but they do not have to be tended to. Just stir occasionally.*

- *Tasso is a highly seasoned, intensely flavored smoked pork used in Cajun cuisine. There is really no good substitute. It is available in specialty food stores and by mail order . . . and, of course, everywhere in Louisiana!*

Shrimp and Grits

There are many versions of this recipe. I prefer the tasso gravy over the usual bacon and mushroom sauce.

GRITS: In a 3-quart saucepan, bring chicken broth and half-and-half to a boil. Stir in grits and continue to stir occasionally until broth is absorbed and grits are soft . . . about 20 to 25 minutes. Stir in heavy cream and continue to cook. Season with salt and pepper. Grits should be "fluffy." If they become too stiff, add water. If fact, if you have time, the more water you add, the better . . . about 1/2 cup at a time and cook down before adding more. They just get fluffier.

TASSO GRAVY: In a 2-quart saucepan, melt butter, add tasso and onion and sauté briefly. Stir in flour and cook over medium heat to lightly brown. Increase heat and add chicken broth. Whisk to combine and stir until thickened. Reduce heat and simmer for 10 to 15 minutes.

SHRIMP AND SAUSAGE: Preheat oven to 400 degrees. Pierce sides of sausage with a fork and place on baking sheet. Bake for 10 to 15 minutes or until cooked and juices run clear. Cool and cut into bite-size pieces.

Heat olive oil in sauté pan. Add cooked sausage and brown lightly. Add shrimp and sauté until they just begin to turn pink. Add tasso gravy and simmer for 1 or 2 minutes.

TO SERVE: Place hot grits on plate. Top with shrimp and sausage mixture. Garnish with chopped parsley.

GRITS
4 cups chicken broth
2 cups half-and-half
2 cups grits
1 cup heavy cream
salt and pepper to taste

TASSO GRAVY
4 tablespoons butter
1 cup tasso, small dice
1 cup chopped onion
1/2 cup flour
4 cups chicken broth

SHRIMP AND SAUSAGE
3/4 pound Edwards smoked link sausage
1 tablespoon olive oil
2 pounds raw shrimp, shelled and deveined

parsley, chopped (garnish)

Brunch Casserole

SERVES 8 TO 10

CREAM SAUCE: Melt butter in a large saucepan over medium heat; add flour and next 5 ingredients. Cook, stirring often, until creamy. Add cheese, stirring until melted. Set aside.

CASSEROLE: Place 8 sliced eggs in the bottom of a 9×13×2-inch baking dish. Layer with 1/3 each of bacon, parsley, and cream sauce. Repeat layers twice using remaining egg, bacon, parsley, and sauce.

Combine topping ingredients. Spread over casserole. Bake in preheated 350-degree oven for 30 minutes or until casserole is hot.

CREAM SAUCE
1/3 cup butter
1/4 cup flour
pinch of salt
1 cup heavy cream
1 cup milk
1/2 teaspoon dried basil
1/2 teaspoon dried thyme
1 pound sharp Cheddar cheese, grated

CASSEROLE
2 dozen hard-cooked eggs, sliced
1 pound bacon, diced and cooked
1/4 cup chopped fresh parsley

TOPPING
1/2 cup panko (Japanese bread crumbs)
1/4 cup freshly grated Parmesan cheese
1 teaspoon dried thyme
1/2 teaspoon dried basil
1/4 teaspoon salt
freshly ground black pepper

Hash Brown and Sausage Casserole

In an iron skillet, sauté country sausage, breaking it up as it cooks. Drain on paper towels. Add smoked sausage pieces to skillet and cook. Drain and combine with country sausage.

Combine hash browns and green onions with sausage. Combine eggs, evaporated milk, cheese, salt, and pepper. Pour over potato and sausage mixture. Transfer to greased 3-quart flat casserole. Top with 1/2 cup cheese. Bake in preheated 350-degree oven for 30 to 45 minutes or mixture is set in the center.

1 pound hot or mild country sausage
1/2 pound smoked sausage, sliced and quartered

1 pound frozen diced hash brown potatoes, thawed
1/2 cup green onions, sliced

4 eggs
17 ounces evaporated milk
1 cup Cheddar cheese
1/2 teaspoon salt
freshly ground black pepper

1/2 cup Cheddar cheese (topping)

TEACHING NOTES

Brunch Casserole

- *When a recipe calls for diced cooked bacon, cut raw bacon into small pieces while bacon is very cold. No need to separate the pieces. Just put them in your skillet and cook slowly over low to medium heat until pieces are separated, cooked and crisp. Stir occasionally. Drain and use.*

- *Egg slicers are obviously a great tool to use in this recipe but they are also an asset when chopped eggs are needed for tuna salad, egg salad, etc. To chop an egg using an egg slicer, slice egg with slicer then carefully turn egg 180 degrees and slice again. Voila! Chopped eggs!*

- *Cooked sausage can be substituted for the bacon. Neese's Hot Sausage would work great.*

Hash Brown and Sausage Casserole

- *I have done this casserole with so many different ingredients. Add fresh herbs such as basil or sage. Want a little green? Add frozen spinach that has been thawed and squeezed dry. And sautéed mushrooms are not out of the question.*

- *Get the picture? This is just a starting point for your imagination.*

123

TEACHING NOTES

French Toast Casserole

- *For an even richer casserole, use brioche instead of French bread. And the apple-cinnamon syrup from Stonewall Kitchens is a great substitute for the maple syrup. Serve with fresh fruit. Or tuck fresh blueberries in and around the layers of bread before baking.*

- *Always use freshly grated nutmeg. Whole nutmeg keeps forever. The already ground variety has a very short shelf life. You know the test . . . if it has no smell, it has no taste. Now, just how old are those spices in your cabinet?*

Pain Perdu aux Pruneaux et Lardons

SERVES 8

That sounds a lot better than Bread Casserole with Prunes and Bacon! You must try it . . . so much better than the typical breakfast casserole.

Cut rye bread into 2×1/2-inch strips . . . small batons. Place in greased 3-quart casserole. Blanch diced bacon in boiling water for a minute or so. Drain. Scatter bacon, parsley, and prunes over bread.

Whisk together eggs and egg yolks with half-and-half, nutmeg, salt, and pepper. Pour over bread mixture. Top with Parmesan cheese. Bake in preheated 375-oven for 30 minutes or until set.

8 slices rye bread (6 or 7 cups)
6 slices bacon, diced
1/3 cup parsley
20 pitted prunes

2 whole eggs
2 egg yolks
1 quart half-and-half
1/2 teaspoon freshly grated nutmeg
1/2 teaspoon salt
freshly ground pepper

1/2 cup freshly grated
   Parmesan cheese

French Toast Casserole

SERVES 8 TO 10

This is a recipe used many times for breakfast caterings. It always got rave reviews.

Cut French bread into 1-inch slices. Arrange the slices in 2 rows in a buttered 9×13-inch baking dish, overlapping the slices. Combine the eggs, half-and-half, milk, sugar, vanilla, cinnamon, nutmeg, and salt in a bowl. Beat or whisk until blended. Pour evenly over the bread slices, spooning some of the mixture in between the slices. Chill, covered, overnight.

TOPPING: Combine the butter, brown sugar, pecans, corn syrup, cinnamon and nutmeg in a bowl and mix well. Spread over the bread mixture. Bake at 350 degrees for 40 minutes or until puffed and light brown. Serve with maple syrup.

1 (13- to 16-ounce) loaf
   French bread

8 eggs
2 cups half-and-half
1 cup milk
2 tablespoons sugar
1 teaspoon vanilla extract
1/4 teaspoon cinnamon
1/4 teaspoon freshly grated nutmeg
dash of salt

TOPPING
1 cup butter, room temperature
1 cup packed light brown sugar
1 cup pecans, chopped
2 tablespoons light corn syrup
1/2 teaspoon cinnamon
1/2 teaspoon freshly grated nutmeg

maple syrup

Pasta & Pizza

▶ *. . . the vehicle for what you have on hand. Let these recipes be a guide for your own creations.*

MARY JAMES

Pasta & Pizza

at a glance

Greek Pasta with Seafood

SERVES 8

Lee Wooding taught this recipe years ago. It became a staple in the cooking school at Roosters.

Prep ingredients as indicated in ingredient list. Set aside. Cook pasta al dente. Drain, rinse and drain again. Immediately toss in large bowl with olive oil. Add prepped ingredients. Add seafood. Refrigerate for at least one hour for best flavor.

TO SERVE: Line large flat serving bowl with romaine or leafy lettuce. Heap on pasta, garnish with fresh herb cuttings i.e., basil, oregano, chive blossoms, etc.

1 (12- to 16-ounce) package dried fettuccine or strozzapreti
3/4 cup olive oil

3 cloves garlic, minced
2/3 cup each crumbled feta cheese and freshly grated Parmesan cheese
3 tablespoons chopped fresh oregano (or 1 tablespoon dried)
3 tablespoons chopped fresh basil (or 1 tablespoon dried)
3/4 cup green olives, drained and chopped
3/4 cup kalamata olives, drained and chopped
3/4 cup chopped green onions
1 cup chopped bell pepper (red, green or combination)
1/2 cup fresh parsley, chopped

3/4 pound shrimp, steamed and cooled
1/2 pound bay scallops, steamed and cooled

salt and freshly ground black pepper

Sesame Noodles

SERVES 6 TO 8

Combine tahini with warm water using a whisk. Add soy sauce, vegetable oil, hoisin, honey, vinegar, sesame oil, garlic, and red pepper flakes. Whisk to combine.

Gently toss spaghetti with tahini mixture. Sprinkle with green onions, bell pepper, and carrots. Garnish with sesame seeds. Serve.

VARIATIONS: Thaw and rinse edamame (soy beans) and add to pasta. Or add snow peas which have been julienned and blanched then rinsed in cold water.

1 pound dry spaghetti, cooked

1/4 cup tahini
1/4 cup warm water
1/4 cup soy sauce
1/4 cup vegetable oil
2 tablespoons each hoisin sauce, honey and cider vinegar
2 teaspoons oriental sesame oil
2 cloves garlic, minced
1/4 teaspoon red pepper flakes

1 cup sliced green onions
1 red bell pepper, diced
2 medium carrots, small dice

2 or 3 tablespoons sesame seeds, toasted

PASTA · PIZZA

TEACHING NOTES

Greek Pasta with Seafood

This recipe was always used in the cooking school when we wanted to talk about fresh vs. dried herbs. The recipe is excellent with either but each way has its own individual taste. Of course, you can use all shrimp, or all scallops. For individual servings, I do not add the seafood to the pasta. Instead, I mound the pasta in an individual flat pasta bowl and top with the larger sea scallops that I have seasoned with salt and pepper and pan seared in olive oil.

Sesame Noodles

This recipe is easily increased and works well for a buffet presentation. Mound pasta on large flat platter and surround with grilled shrimp or sliced grilled chicken or pork tenderloin.

TEACHING NOTES

Tortellini with Fresh Fruit & Blue Cheese

- *Pick up a fruit variety pack in the produce department of your grocery store. Feel comfortable with changing the fruit selection. Bananas are good but remember they discolor quickly.*

- *This makes a great luncheon dish on a bed of lettuce banked by slices of grilled chicken.*

Penne with Lemon, Capers, Olives & Arugula

SERVES 4 TO 6

Add 1 tablespoon salt to large amount of water. Bring to a boil. Cook pasta until al dente.

Heat olive oil in sauté pan over medium heat. Add lemon slices and cook for several minutes. Lemon edges should begin to brown. Add garlic, olives, and capers. Bring to a simmer and cook another minute.

Drain pasta. Add arugula. Pour on hot olive oil mixture. Toss to coat. Season with salt and freshly ground black pepper. Serve

VARIATION: Mound steamed shrimp on top of each serving.

1 tablespoon salt
8 ounces small penne or
   strozzapreti pasta

3/4 cup extra-virgin olive oil
1 lemon, sliced very thin
   and quartered

1 tablespoon minced garlic
3/4 cup pitted kalamatas, chopped
2 tablespoons capers, drained
7 ounces arugula
salt and freshly ground black pepper

Tortellini with Fresh Fruit & Blue Cheese

SERVES 8 AS SIDE DISH

A unique pasta salad.

Cook tortellini according to package directions. Drain.

Combine strawberries, pineapple, kiwi, and 1/2 cup of the toasted walnuts. Set aside while preparing sauce.

BLUE CHEESE SAUCE: Combine mayonnaise, sour cream, yogurt, and blue cheese. Season with black pepper to taste.

ASSEMBLY: Add fruit and Blue Cheese Sauce to tortellini. Toss very gently to combine. Just before serving, garnish with fresh raspberries and remaining 1/4 cup toasted walnuts.

2 (7-ounce) boxes tri-colored
   cheese tortellini
1/2 cup strawberries, quartered
1/2 cup fresh pineapple, cut in chunks
1/2 cup sliced and quartered kiwi
3/4 cup walnuts, toasted and
   coarsely chopped

1/2 pint fresh raspberries (garnish)

BLUE CHEESE SAUCE
1/2 cup mayonnaise
1/2 cup sour cream
1/4 cup plain yogurt
8 ounces blue cheese, crumbled
freshly ground black pepper

Penne, Spinach & Proscuitto Gratin

SERVES 8 AS SIDE DISH

Cook pasta according to package directions. Drain and rinse. Add proscuitto, spinach, Parmesan cheese, and basil. Toss to combine. Transfer to a greased 6-cup gratin dish or flat casserole. Set aside.

In a mixing bowl, whisk together cream, egg, olive oil, garlic, salt, and pepper. Pour over pasta mixture. Bake in preheated 350-degree oven for 30 minutes or until mixture has set.

8 ounces dry penne pasta
2 ounces proscuitto, diced
4 cups fresh baby spinach, roughly chopped
1 cup grated Parmesan cheese
1/4 cup fresh basil

2 cups heavy cream
1 egg
2 tablespoons olive oil
1 teaspoon minced garlic
salt and freshly ground black pepper

PASTA · PIZZA

TEACHING NOTES

Penne, Spinach & Proscuitto Gratin

- *Gratins are a great way to use up leftover cooked meats, adding vegetables that you have on hand. They can be assembled ahead, then baked and served in the same dish. Gratin is the French word for the crusty, golden top that forms during baking.*

- *Although Parmesan cheese is called for in the recipe, you could substitute Comté, Cantal, Asiago, or any other hard grating cheese.*

Orzo Salad with Orange Sesame Dressing

SERVES 10

This recipe did not originate with me. It was chosen from a community cookbook as a pasta salad of the week at Roosters. The week became years of popularity.

In large pot of boiling salted water, cook orzo until tender. Drain. Rinse with cold water. Drain well and transfer to large mixing bowl. Toss with sesame oil. Add carrots, raisins, sunflower seeds, parsley and green onions. Toss to combine.

ORANGE SESAME DRESSING: Combine all ingredients in food processor fitted with a steel blade or in a blender. Process until smooth.

TO SERVE: Add dressing to orzo mixture. Mound in large flat pasta bowl. Garnish with orange sections. Sprinkle with parsley.

1 pound orzo
1 tablespoon sesame oil
4 carrots, cut in matchsticks
2 cups raisins
1 cup sunflower seeds
1/4 cup parsley, chopped
1/4 cup sliced green onions

ORANGE SESAME DRESSING
1/2 cup vegetable oil
3 tablespoons rice wine vinegar
3 tablespoons sesame oil
2 tablespoons grated orange peel
2 teaspoons sugar
2 teaspoons minced ginger
1 1/2 teaspoons soy sauce
1 small clove garlic
1 1/2 teaspoons salt
1 teaspoon freshly ground black pepper
1/4 teaspoon red pepper flakes

orange sections (garnish)
chopped parsley (garnish)

Orzo Salad with Orange Sesame Dressing

At Roosters, we always had a bottle of Boyajian Orange Oil. This was used in place of the grated orange peel. It only takes 1/2 teaspoon. This oil is also a great addition to cookies, cakes, and even some poultry dishes. But remember, a little goes a long way!

129

TEACHING NOTES

Puttanesca Sauce

I can hear it now . . . "I don't like anchovies." Don't discount this recipe because of the anchovies. They add a real depth of flavor to the sauce and are not recognizable as anchovies when the sauce is finished.

Cracker Crust Pizza
Suggested Toppings

- *Brie cheese pieces, pine nuts, diced tomatoes, and fresh basil*

- *Thin layer of mayonnaise, diced cooked bacon, diced fresh tomatoes, and minced fresh parsley or basil*

- *Truffle oil, sautéed mushrooms, thinly sliced cooked potatoes, and Reblochon cheese*

- *Cambozola cheese pieces or blue cheese, walnuts, and fresh basil*

Puttanesca Sauce

SERVES 4 WITH PASTA

Dress up your favorite jarred marinara sauce for an easy dinner. Named for the Naples "ladies of the night," this sauce is so quick to prepare that it could be done between clients.

In a 2-quart saucepan, heat olive oil. Add garlic and anchovy fillets. Cook gently and stir until anchovies are dissolved. Add marinara sauce, olives, capers, and parsley. Simmer for 5 to 10 minutes. Use with your favorite cooked pasta.

3 tablespoons olive oil
2 tablespoons minced garlic
6 anchovy fillets, drained, chopped

1 (17-ounce) jar marinara sauce

1/2 cup oil-cured black olives or kalamatas, chopped
1/4 cup capers
1/2 cup parsley, chopped

Cracker Crust Pizza

MAKES 1 PIZZA

CRUST: Combine flour, yeast, and salt. Add water and olive oil. Stir to combine then turn out onto floured board and knead until smooth and elastic. Place in oiled bowl and let rise until doubled in bulk. When ready to use, punch down and roll out to 1/8-inch thickness in desired shape.

Transfer to pizza peel that has been sprinkled heavily with cornmeal. Choose toppings (left).

TO TRANSFER PIZZA: Shake the peel to make sure pizza is loose. Holding the peel at a 20-degree angle, place the front tip on the back side of the baking stone. Make short, gentle, back and forth jerking motions with the pizza peel causing the pizza to slide off the peel as the peel is pulled away.

TO BAKE: Place pizza stone in oven and preheat to 450 degrees. Using the method above, transfer pizza to preheated stone. Bake for 10 to 12 minutes or until crust is crisp and toppings are cooked. If convection is used, cooking time will be less.

CRUST
2 cups flour
2 teaspoons Saf Instant Yeast or Rapid-Rise yeast
1/2 teaspoon salt

3/4 cup warm water
3 tablespoons olive oil

Smoked Salmon & Caper Pizza

MAKES 1 PIZZA

Pizza is just a vehicle for your favorite toppings. Use it as an appetizer, a side to a salad or soup, or as a main dish.

Prepare pizza crust as directed in recipe. Place crust on cornmeal dusted pizza peel. Rub or brush with olive oil. Evenly distribute goat cheese over pizza. Dot with pieces of salmon. Top with red onion, capers, and Parmesan cheese. Transfer to stone in preheated 425-degree oven and bake for 15 to 20 minutes. Remove from oven and immediately zest the lemon overall. Sprinkle with herbs and drizzle lightly with olive oil. Serve.

1 recipe Cracker Crust Pizza dough (page 130)

TOPPING
6 ounces goat cheese
smoked presliced salmon
red onion, small dice
capers, drained
Parmesan cheese, grated

zest of 1 lemon
fresh dill, chopped
fresh parsley, chopped
olive oil

PASTA · PIZZA

Smoked Salmon & Caper Pizza

- *A convection oven is not necessary but certainly creates a better product. If using convection, use the same oven temperature but reduce the cooking time.*

- *Don't have a pizza peel or stone? Use a traditional pizza pan. Cooking time will be longer. Bake until crust is browned on edges.*

Mediterranean Phyllo Pizza

MAKES 12 (4-INCH SQUARE) PIECES

This was always a good way to introduce phyllo to the novice cook. As a crust for pizza, layering does not have to be so exact.

Drain tomatoes. Split each tomato and place in sieve then spread on paper towels to absorb liquid. Slice eggplant into 1/4- or 1/2-inch slices. Drizzle lightly with olive oil and grill or pan sauté until done.

Unroll phyllo and working quickly layer 9 sheets of phyllo on 11×17-inch baking sheet brushing olive oil between each piece of phyllo and sprinkling Parmesan cheese between each layer. Roll edges to finish. Dot crust with tomatoes, and then eggplant, garlic, basil, and feta cheese. Bake in preheated 400-degree oven for 20 to 30 minutes or until golden.

1 (28-ounce) can whole tomatoes
1 eggplant, peeled
2 heads garlic, roasted
fresh basil, chiffonade
feta cheese or soft goat cheese

1 package phyllo sheets, thawed
1/2 cup grated Parmesan cheese
1/3 cup extra-virgin olive oil

Mediterranean Phyllo Pizza

- *Roasted Garlic: Leaving root end of garlic intact, cut off other end exposing tips of cloves. Place on microwave-safe and ovenproof dish, cut side up. Drizzle with olive oil. Cover with plastic wrap. Microwave on high for 1 1/2 to 2 minutes. Remove plastic wrap and bake in preheated 350-degree oven for 20 to 30 minutes. Let stand until cool. Squeeze to remove cloves.*

- *Variations on this recipe abound. Just think of all the flavors of the Mediterranean . . . France, Spain, Italy, Greece . . . then add your own personal touch. I usually add oil-cured or kalamata olives. Don't have fresh basil? Substitute 2 teaspoons of herbes de Provence, etc.*

131

TEACHING NOTES

The dough for this torta is extremely user-friendly. It was the dough used for the famous Roosters on the Run Chicken Potpie. After making the torta once, you will understand the recipe and be able to cut your preparation time in half. It can be done 2 or 3 days ahead.

Can store for several days refrigerated. Reheat in preheated 350-degree oven for 20 to 30 minutes. Serve slightly warm or at room temperature. If made ahead, take out of the refrigerator a couple of hours before reheating.

Torta Rustica

SERVES 16 TO 20

Nick Malgieri taught many classes at Roosters. This is an adaptation of his torta as it appears in his book How to Bake. *Thank you, Nick, for all you have taught us.*

DOUGH: Combine dry ingredients in bowl of food processor and pulse several times. Cut butter into 10 pieces and distribute evenly over dry ingredients. Pulse until very finely powdered. Add eggs and continue to pulse until dough forms a ball. Add 1 to 2 tablespoons water if necessary. Divide dough into 2 pieces, one of which is 2/3 of the dough and the other is 1/3 of the dough. Press large piece into a round disk and smaller piece into a square. Wrap and chill.

FILLING: In a very large mixing bowl, mix eggs into ricotta. Add mozzarella cheese, Asiago cheese, salami, roasted peppers, basil, parsley, and fennel seeds and stir.

ASSEMBLY: Preheat oven to 350 degrees and set a rack in the lower third of oven. Roll larger piece into a 17-inch circle to line a 12-inch straight-sided cake, deep-dish pizza or springform pan. Pour in filling and smooth top. Roll the remaining dough to a 12-inch square and cut into 1-inch strips. Arrange 6 strips on filling. Arrange remaining strips at a 45-degree angle to first ones. Roll edges over to enclose strips . . . making sure that there is no overlap on the sides of the pan (makes it easier to remove torta from pan later). Brush with egg wash.

Bake for 45 minutes or until filling is set and slightly puffed. Cool in the pan on a rack. To unmold, place the back side of a sheet pan on the torta and invert. Remove baking pan. Now, place serving platter on top of torta, invert again so that torta is right side up.

EGG WASH: Mix all the ingredients.

DOUGH
3 cups flour
2 tablespoons sugar
1 teaspoon baking powder
1/2 teaspoon salt

3/4 cup butter

3 eggs

FILLING
6 eggs
2 pounds ricotta cheese
1 pound mozzarella cheese, grated
1/2 pound Asiago cheese, grated
1/2 pound sopressata or Genoa salami, small dice
1/4 cup roasted red peppers, drained and chopped
1/2 cup fresh basil, chopped
1/2 cup fresh parsley, chopped
1 teaspoon fennel seeds

EGG WASH
1 egg
pinch salt
1 tablespoon water

Desserts

▶ *. . . Desserts may be stressed spelled backwards but they can be a great stress reliever . . . .*

MARY JAMES

DESSERTS

Desserts

at a glance

Fresh Apple Walnut Cake with Brown Sugar Glaze

SERVES 8 TO 12

DESSERTS

This recipe made the rounds in Martinsville, Virginia, and came to Roosters on the Run through a friend. It was one our most popular desserts.

Preheat oven to 350 degrees.

In a large mixing bowl, whisk eggs and then add vegetable oil and sugar. Combine.

Stir together flour, baking soda, and salt. Stir into egg mixture. Add walnuts and vanilla. Combine. Finally, add apples and mix well. Pour into a greased and floured 9×13-inch baking pan. Bake for 25 to 30 minutes. Remove from oven and immediately prick with a toothpick and evenly distribute glaze.

GLAZE: In a small saucepan, combine glaze ingredients. Bring to a boil and cook for 2 minutes.

TO SERVE: Cut into squares and serve with vanilla ice cream if desired.

3 eggs
1 1/2 cups vegetable oil
2 cups sugar

3 cups flour
1 teaspoon baking soda
1/2 teaspoon salt

1 cup walnuts or pecans, chopped
2 teaspoons vanilla

3 cups coarsely chopped Granny Smith apples

GLAZE
1 cup light brown sugar
1/2 cup butter
1/4 cup evaporated milk

135

TEACHING NOTES

Martha's Carrot Cake

Friend and partner, Martha Turner, became famous when Nick Malgieri included her carrot cake in his Perfect Cakes *book.*

Preheat oven to 325 degrees.

Stir together flour, baking powder, baking soda, and cinnamon.

In mixer, combine oil and sugar. Add eggs one at a time, beating after each.

Add dry ingredients. Mix well. Add carrots, pineapple, and nuts. Stir to combine.

Grease three 9-inch cake pans with butter then line bottom with parchment paper and butter again. Evenly distribute batter between pans. Transfer to preheated oven and bake for 25 to 30 minutes.

ICING: Using a mixer, mix cream cheese and butter. Add vanilla and confectioners' sugar Beat until smooth. Ice tops and side of cake.

2 cups flour
2 teaspoons baking powder
1 1/2 teaspoons baking soda
2 teaspoons cinnamon

1 1/2 cups vegetable oil
2 cups sugar
4 eggs

2 cups grated carrots (about 4 large)
1 (8-ounce) can crushed pineapple
   and juice
3/4 cup pecans, chopped

ICING
12 ounces cream cheese
3/4 cup butter, room temperature

1 tablespoon vanilla
6 cups confectioners' sugar, sifted
   after measuring

Pumpkin Roll

TEACHING NOTES

Hundreds of these cakes were made in the Roosters on the Run kitchen during the fall of the year, especially at Thanksgiving.

Preheat oven to 375 degrees.

Prepare an 18×13-inch half sheet pan. Grease pan with shortening. Line bottom with parchment paper and grease and flour paper. Set aside.

Using a mixer, combine pumpkin, eggs, and sugar. Beat until well combined.

In a separate bowl, stir together flour, baking soda, salt, cinnamon, ginger, and nutmeg. Add to pumpkin mixture. Beat just to combine. Pour into prepared pan.

Bake in preheated oven for 12 to 15 minutes or until cake springs back when touched.

Cut a piece of parchment paper slightly larger than pan and dust with powdered sugar. While cake is still hot, turn out onto paper and roll up in paper. Allow to cool.

FILLING: Beat together cream cheese, butter, and vanilla. Add powdered sugar and beat to combine.

TO FINISH: Unroll cake. Remove paper. Spread with filling. Roll into jelly roll and place seam side down on pan. Dust with powdered sugar. Refrigerate or freeze.

TO SERVE: Trim crusty ends (treat for the cook). Slice into 1-inch slices and serve dusted with powdered sugar or your favorite jarred caramel sauce, warmed.

1²/₃ cups canned pumpkin

5 eggs

2 cups sugar

1¹/₂ cups flour

2 teaspoons baking soda

1 teaspoon salt

1 teaspoon cinnamon

¹/₂ teaspoon powdered ginger

¹/₂ teaspoon freshly grated nutmeg

FILLING

11 ounces cream cheese

2 tablespoons butter

1 teaspoon vanilla

1¹/₂ cups powdered sugar

137

www.maryjames.net

TEACHING NOTES

*This recipe will seem very strange
and unorthodox when you see the
dough floating in the vinegar and
water. Don't be concerned. It bakes
into an ooey gooey comfort food
dessert. Guests invariably say it
reminds them of something from
their childhood, but no one has
been able to say what it is from
their childhood!*

Butter Rolls

SERVES 6 TO 8

*This is a recipe that my father would
describe to me as "a wonderful butter roll
made with biscuit dough and vinegar." His
description made no sense to me. However,
after much research, I think this is it.*

Using your fingertips or a pastry blender,
cut shortening into flour until the texture
of coarse cornmeal. Add buttermilk all
at once. Quickly mix together. Divide in
half. Roll each half on a floured surface
into a rectangle that is about 1/4 inch
thick. Spread each with half the melted
butter then sprinkle each with half the
brown sugar and cinnamon. Roll up like
a jelly roll beginning at the long side.
Cut into 1-inch slices. Place cut sides
up in a greased 9-inch square pan.

Pour vinegar and water over the rolls.
Pour sugar over top and dot with butter.
Bake in preheated 350-degree oven for
45 minutes to 1 hour. Serve warm with
whipped cream or ice cream. Drizzle
with extra sauce.

BISCUIT DOUGH
3 cups self-rising flour
6 tablespoons shortening

1 1/2 cups buttermilk

6 tablespoons butter, melted
2/3 cup brown sugar
1 1/2 teaspoons cinnamon

SAUCE
2/3 cup cider vinegar
2 cups water
1 cup sugar
1/2 cup butter

138

Blackberry Cobbler

SERVES 8

Heavily butter a flat 2-quart baking dish. Gently toss blackberries with sugar and transfer to prepared dish. Sprinkle flour over the berries. Dot with butter; set aside.

CRUST: Sift flour with sugar, baking powder, salt, and cream of tartar. Cut in butter until mixture resembles coarse meal. Add milk all at once and stir to form into a ball. On a floured board, roll dough to 1/4-inch thickness and in the shape of the baking dish allowing an extra inch all around. Place dough directly on the berries with extra dough "crawling" up the sides. With your fingers, carefully roll this extra dough to form an edge on the crust, gently pressing it to the inside of the dish. Cut a vent in the center of the dough and sprinkle top with 2 or 3 tablespoons sugar.

Bake in 400-degree oven for 40 minutes, or until crust is golden. Serve warm with vanilla ice cream.

5 cups fresh blackberries
1 cup sugar
3 tablespoons flour
4 tablespoons butter

CRUST
2 cups flour
2 tablespoons sugar
4 teaspoons baking powder
1/2 teaspoon salt
1/2 teaspoon cream of tartar
1/2 cup butter

1/2 cup milk

2 or 3 tablespoons sugar

vanilla ice cream

TEACHING NOTES

Crumbly Peach Pie

MAKES ONE 9-INCH PIE

Carolyn Pokela is well known in Greensboro for her pie-making abilities. This made-in-the-pie plate summertime treat is one of her favorites and ours, too.

Preheat oven to 400 degrees.

CRUST: In a 9-inch pie plate or pan, combine flour, sugar, and salt. Whisk together oil and milk. Add to flour mixture in pan. Combine and using fingertips press crust across the bottom and up sides of pie plate or pan.

FILLING: Cut peaches in half and pit. Evenly arrange 8 halves over crust, pit side up. Combine butter, flour, and sugar until crumbly and scatter over peaches. Sprinkle with 4 tablespoons water.

Transfer to preheated oven and bake for 40 to 50 minutes.

CRUST
1 1/2 cups flour
1 1/2 teaspoons sugar
1/2 teaspoon salt

1/2 cup vegetable oil
2 tablespoons cold milk

FILLING
4 fresh peaches, peeled

1/4 cup butter
1/3 cup flour
1 cup sugar
4 tablespoons water

TEACHING NOTES

Caramel Heavenlies

If the bars become too hard to remove from pan, return to the oven for 2 or 3 minutes to soften. Once you get a corner lifted up, you will be able to easily cut between the squares.

Brownies with White Chocolate & Cranberries

MAKES 18 TO 24 PIECES

Lucy Hamilton taught many classes at Roosters. Her desserts are always extraordinary and these brownies are an all-time favorite.

Preheat oven to 350 degrees.

Melt butter and unsweetened chocolate together. Stir in sugar. Cool to lukewarm.

Add beaten eggs, almond extract, and vanilla to chocolate mixture. Mix well to combine. Add flour. Stir in pecans, white chocolate, and cranberries.

Pour into greased 9×13-inch pan. Transfer to preheated oven and bake for 30 minutes. Cool, cut into squares.

1 cup butter
4 ounces unsweetened chocolate, chopped
2 cups sugar

4 eggs, beaten
1/4 teaspoon almond extract
1/2 teaspoon vanilla extract

1 cup flour

1 cup pecans, chopped
1 cup white chocolate chips
1/2 cup dried cranberries, chopped

Caramel Heavenlies

MAKES 30 TO 36 PIECES

I first saw this recipe in a South Carolina Junior League cookbook. Some of our best recipes come from these community cookbooks.

Arrange graham crackers in a single layer in a 10×15-inch jelly roll pan. Sprinkle with marshmallows.

Combine the butter, brown sugar, and cinnamon in a saucepan. Cook over medium heat until the brown sugar dissolves, stirring constantly. Remove from heat. Stir in the vanilla. Drizzle over the marshmallows; sprinkle with the almonds and coconut.

Bake at 350 degrees for 12 to 14 minutes or until light brown. Cool in pan on a wire rack. Cut into 3-inch squares; cut each square into halves to form triangles.

Store in airtight container in refrigerator for up to 2 weeks or freeze for up to 3 months.

12 double graham crackers
2 cups miniature marshmallows
3/4 cup butter
3/4 cup brown sugar
1 teaspoon cinnamon
1 teaspoon vanilla
1 cup sliced almonds
1 cup flaked coconut

140

Cappuccino Thins

This Lucy Hamilton recipe is the best slice-and-bake cookie I have ever had!

In food processor fitted with a steel blade, process chocolate chips, sugar, brown sugar, egg yolk, espresso powder, cocoa, and cinnamon until chocolate is in small pieces. Add butter and process for 45 seconds to 1 minute. Add flour and pulse just until flour is incorporated.

Remove dough from processor bowl. Shape into 1 1/2-inch logs. Wrap in plastic wrap and refrigerate for at least 1 hour.

Preheat oven to 375 degrees. Slice cookies about 1/8 inch thick and place on pan lined with parchment or reusable pan liner. Transfer to preheated oven and bake for about 10 to 12 minutes. Cool on wire rack.

Place the melted chocolate in squeeze bottle with small opening. With cookies on the cooling rack, hold the bottle high over the cookies and use wide sweeping motion back and forth to drizzle chocolate onto cookies.

2 ounces chocolate chips

5 tablespoons sugar

1/4 cup brown sugar

1 egg yolk

1 1/2 teaspoon instant espresso powder

1 1/2 teaspoon cocoa

1/2 teaspoon cinnamon

1/2 cup butter, cut into 8 pieces

1 cup flour

1/2 cup chocolate chips, melted and cooled to lukewarm

TEACHING NOTES

**White Chocolate
Chunk Cookies**

*Ice cream scoops come in many
different sizes. The size is printed
on the blade, the bowl, or the handle.
Frequently, foodservice scoops come
with different colored handles which
relate to their size. A #16 scoop
holds 1/4 cup and has a blue handle.
Using a scoop creates uniform
cookies, muffins, crab cakes, etc.*

Roosters Chocolate Cookie

*The typical squares of semisweet
chocolate can be used. However,
bittersweet makes a richer, more
chocolaty cookie. I have even used
a 70% chocolate. Now that's a
chocolate cookie!*

White Chocolate Chunk Cookies

MAKES 16 GIANT COOKIES

Preheat oven to 375 degrees. Combine
flour, baking soda, and salt. Set aside.

In mixer, combine butter, sugars, and
vanilla. Beat until well combined and
creamy. Beat in eggs. Add flour mixture.
Stir in white chocolate and nuts. Using a
#16 ice cream scoop, place level scoops
on pan lined with parchment or a reusable
pan liner . . . 6 scoops per pan. Bake for
10 to 12 minutes.

VARIATION: Add the zest of
one orange.

- 2 2/3 cups flour
- 1 teaspoon baking soda
- 1 teaspoon salt

- 1 cup butter
- 3/4 cup sugar
- 3/4 cup packed brown sugar
- 1 teaspoon vanilla

- 2 eggs

- 1 1/2 cups coarsely chopped
  white chocolate
- 1 cup macadamia nuts, toasted,
  coarsely chopped

Roosters Chocolate Cookie

MAKES 20 TO 22 LARGE COOKIES

*Okay, here it is . . . the Roosters on the
Run Chocolate Cookie! This cookie was
on the cover of* Bon Appétit *magazine the
month after we opened Roosters.*

Melt chocolate in double boiler. Add
butter. Stir until butter is melted.
Remove from heat. Cool to lukewarm.

Combine flour, baking powder, and
salt. Using mixer, beat eggs and brown
sugar until thick. Reduce speed and add
chocolate mixture. Add flour mixture
and mix. Add toffee pieces and pecans.
Mix just to combine. Chill batter for
15 to 20 minutes.

Preheat oven to 350 degrees. Line cookie
sheets with parchment paper or reusable
pan liner. Using a #16 ice cream scoop
(1/4 cup scoop), drop scoops onto baking
sheet. Bake for about 15 minutes Cookies
are done when tops are crackled but still
soft. Cool on pan.

- 1 pound bittersweet chocolate,
  cut in pieces
- 4 tablespoons butter

- 1/2 cup flour
- 1 teaspoon baking powder
- 1/2 teaspoon salt

- 4 eggs
- 1 3/4 cups packed light brown sugar
- 2 teaspoons vanilla

- 8 ounces Heath Bar toffee pieces
- 1 cup pecans, chopped

Tuiles

These cookies are reminiscent of the roof tiles of the Mediterranean.

zest of 1 orange
6 tablespoons orange juice
1 1/4 cups sugar

3/4 cup flour
1 1/2 cups sliced almonds
1/2 cup butter, melted and cooled

Combine zest, juice, and sugar in a small bowl. Add flour and almonds. Stir in melted butter. Chill batter for at least 1 hour.

Preheat oven to 400 degrees. Line baking sheet with a reusable pan liner such as a Silpat. Drop heaping teaspoonfuls onto lined pan at least 3 inches apart. Bake for 5 to 8 minutes or until edges begin to brown and center is golden. Remove from oven. Pull pan liner from pan. Allow to cool for 15 to 20 seconds. With a spatula, remove each cookie and drape across a rolling pin to form a curved cookie. If cookies become too cool and won't drape, place back in oven for a few seconds to soften.

Serve plain as is . . . or fill with berries and freshly whipped cream.

TEACHING NOTES

Basil Sorbet

MAKES 3 TO 4 CUPS

Top with fresh sweetened strawberries for a dessert. Scoop into Strawberry Soup (page 40) for a first course . . . or perhaps it could be for dessert . . . your choice.

2 ounces fresh basil
2 1/2 cups water
1 1/2 cups sugar

3 tablespoons lime juice

Remove large stems from basil. In a small saucepan, combine water, sugar, and fresh basil. Bring to a simmer and cook just until sugar is dissolved. Remove from heat. Let stand for 10 minutes. Transfer to blender, blend until smooth. Strain. Add lime juice and freeze according to manufacturer's instructions on ice cream maker.

TEACHING NOTES

Lemon Peel Ice Cream Sandwiches

MAKES 2 QUARTS

With bits of lemon peel scattered through this ice cream, it is a refreshing and perfect ending to a summer meal.

Slice the whole lemon in half lengthwise then each half into very, very thin slices. If lemon is large, then cut slices one more time for small pieces. Remove seeds.

Combine lemon peel and sugar with the juice of 2 lemons. Let stand for at least 3 hours. Just before freezing, add half-and-half. Freeze according to manufacturer's directions on ice cream freezer. Serve as is, or make ice cream sandwiches with chocolate wafer cookies.

TO MAKE ICE CREAM SANDWICHES: Buy chocolate wafer cookies. Allow ice cream to soften just a bit. Place scoop on wafer. Top with second wafer and gently press. Wrap neatly in plastic wrap then in colorful napkins with bow. Store in freezer. Pile in a basket to serve.

I whole lemon

1 1/2 cups sugar
juice of 2 lemons

4 cups half-and-half

plain chocolate wafer cookies

Strawberry Margarita
Frozen Torte

SERVES 8 TO 10

TEACHING NOTES

Excellent do-ahead summertime dessert. Great after a spicy meal.

Butter a 9-inch springform pan. Combine graham cracker crumbs with sugar and melted butter. Press onto bottom and sides of prepared pan. Set aside.

In food processor, combine strawberries, sugar, sweetened condensed milk, tequila, Triple Sec, lime juice, and lime zest. Purée.

In a mixing bowl, whip cream until stiff peaks form. Gently fold whipped cream into strawberry mixture. Pour into prepared crust.

Cover and freeze overnight. Run a sharp knife around the edge of the pan to loosen. Release sides. Cut and serve. Garnish with cut up fresh strawberries if desired.

2 cups graham cracker crumbs
1/3 cup sugar
1/2 cup butter, melted

2 cups fresh strawberries
1/4 cup sugar
3/4 cup sweetened condensed milk
1/2 cup tequila
1/3 cup Triple Sec or orange liqueur
2 tablespoons fresh lime juice
zest of 1 lime

2 cups heavy cream

fresh strawberries (garnish)

TEACHING NOTES

- *The bakery departments of large supermarkets have oversized croissants. These are less expensive and perfect for this recipe. Once you have done this recipe the first time, and understand the logistics, it will become part of your repertoire.*

- *Semisweet chocolate could be substituted for bittersweet. It is only slightly sweeter.*

- *To scrape a vanilla bean, take the tip of a paring knife and split bean. Open and scrape using the blade of the knife.*

- *Water bath tips: Transfer pan with baking dish to oven before filling with water. Once cooked, lift baking dish from hot water and leave water in oven until cool and safe to remove.*

Chocolate Croissant Bread Pudding with Banana

SERVES 8

Lisa Johnson first taught this recipe in a Lunch & Learn class at Roosters. It has become a mainstay in many households in Greensboro.

Preheat oven to 325 degrees. Cut croissants into 1-inch cubes. Place on baking sheet and bake for 10 to 15 minutes or lightly browned. Transfer to greased 9×13-inch casserole. Tuck chocolate pieces and banana slices in and around the bread cubes. Set aside.

Meanwhile, combine cream with scrapings from vanilla bean in a heavy bottomed 2- or 3-quart saucepan. Drop in vanilla bean. Bring to a simmer over medium heat. Remove from heat. Discard vanilla bean pod before proceeding.

In a bowl, whisk egg yolks and sugar to blend. Gradually add hot cream to egg yolks and sugar. Pour custard over bread cubes and chocolate.

Place dish on baking sheet with sides. Place in preheated oven. Carefully add water to the baking pan to come halfway up the sides of the pan. Bake for 40 minutes or until set. Lift carefully from water bath. Serve warm.

4 large croissants
8 ounces bittersweet chocolate, coarsely chopped
1 large banana, sliced

2 cups heavy cream
1 vanilla bean, split lengthwise
5 large egg yolks
3/4 cup sugar

White Chocolate Cream with Fresh Berries

SERVES 6 TO 8

Layer fresh berries with chocolate cream in a sparkling crystal bowl for a delectable presentation.

1^3/$_4$ cups heavy cream, divided
^{1}/$_2$ pound white chocolate

blackberries, blueberries,
   strawberries, raspberries
fresh mint (garnish)

Combine ^{3}/$_4$ cup of the cream with the white chocolate in a double boiler. Do not overheat. Heat just to melt. Remove from double boiler and allow to cool for 30 to 45 minutes. Mixture will be just beginning to thicken.

Whip remaining 1 cup of cream to stiff peaks. Fold into cooled white chocolate mixture.

Layer berries and white chocolate cream in bowl finishing with berries. Or layer in parfait glasses finishing with berries. Garnish with fresh mint.

Panna Cotta with Fresh Blackberries

SERVES 8

In a medium bowl, soften gelatin in 1 tablespoon cold water.

Combine cream, sugar, and vanilla in a small saucepan. Heat just until sugar dissolves. Add softened gelatin. Stir to dissolve. Add buttermilk.

Divide mixture between 8 ungreased 6-ounce ramekins and refrigerate until set. Garnish with blackberries and surround with blackberry syrup.

1 envelope unflavored gelatin
1 tablespoon cold water

1^1/$_4$ cups heavy cream
^{1}/$_2$ cup sugar
^{1}/$_2$ vanilla pod, split lengthwise

1^3/$_4$ cups buttermilk

fresh blackberries
blackberry syrup

Chocolate Decadence

SERVES 12 TO 16

Preheat oven to 425 degrees. Butter an 8-inch cake pan. Line bottom with parchment and butter parchment.

Melt chocolate and butter together in top of double boiler. Remove from heat as soon as melted.

In mixing bowl, whisk eggs with sugar over (not in) simmering water until they just begin to thicken and the sugar is dissolved. When the mixture is lukewarm, it is done. With the electric mixer, whip the eggs until light and fluffy (they will at least triple in volume). Gently fold in flour using a flat roux whisk or spatula.

Add about 1/4 of the egg mixture to the chocolate mixture to lighten. Now pour all the chocolate mixture down the side of the bowl into the egg mixture. Fold together completely, being careful not to overdo. Transfer to prepared pan.

Bake at 425 degrees for 12 to 15 minutes. The middle should jiggle like an undercooked soufflé. Cool in the pan and refrigerate. Freezes well.

RASPBERRY SAUCE: In food processor fitted with a steel blade, purée raspberries. Sweeten to taste with sugar and Chambord. Whip cream and sugar to soft peaks.

TO SERVE: Place a spoonful of raspberry sauce on plate. Top with a sliver of Chocolate Decadence and a dollop of softly whipped cream. Sprinkle with fresh raspberries.

1 pound good-quality semisweet or bittersweet chocolate
5 ounces unsalted butter

4 eggs
1 tablespoon sugar
1 tablespoon flour

RASPBERRY SAUCE
1 pint fresh raspberries
sugar
Chambord liqueur (optional)

1 cup heavy cream
2 tablespoons sugar
fresh raspberries

Coeur a la Crème

SERVES 8

TEACHING NOTES

These wonderful little hearts of cream are a favorite Valentine's Day dessert. It was adapted from The Dione Lucas Book of French Cooking, *circa 1947. Some recipes stand the test of time.*

8 coeur a la crème molds
cheesecloth to fit molds

I cup heavy cream

8 ounces cream cheese
scraping from 1/2 vanilla bean
2/3 cup powdered sugar

SAUCE
2 cups fresh strawberries
1/2 cup seedless raspberry jam
2 tablespoons Chambord liqueur or
   to taste

fresh raspberries
fresh mint

Coeur a la crème molds have holes in the bottom to allow the excess liquid to drain as it chills.

Wet cheesecloth and squeeze dry. Line molds with a single layer of damp cheesecloth, overhanging the edge so mold can be enclosed when filled. Set aside.

Whip cream to soft peaks. Set aside.

With mixer, beat cream cheese until light and fluffy. Add vanilla bean scrapings. Beat in powdered sugar. By hand, stir in whipped cream. Spoon into prepared molds, filling to the top. Close cheesecloth over the top. Place on sheet pan with sides. Cover well and refrigerate for several hours or overnight.

SAUCE: Trim strawberries and cut into bite-size pieces. Melt jam. Add liqueur and pour over strawberries.

TO SERVE: Fold back cheesecloth. Unmold onto serving plate. Carefully remove cheesecloth and surround with sauce. Garnish with a few fresh raspberries and a fresh mint sprig.

DESSERTS

TEACHING NOTES

Chocolate Pâte with Raspberry Sauce

Lining the pan does not have to be difficult. Just turn the pan upside down and place parchment over the pan. Fold down ends as though wrapping a package and tape. Do both ends. Flip pan and put the paper box inside the pan.

Chocolate Pâte with Raspberry Sauce

SERVES 12 TO 16

Line a small straight-sided loaf pan (9×2¹/₂×2 inch) or pâte mold with parchment.

Combine chocolate, wine, and cream in a double boiler or heavy-bottomed saucepan. Cook very gently, being careful not to overheat . . . less than a minute on the heat. Whisk just until chocolate is melted and mixture is smooth. Return to the heat briefly if necessary. Pour into prepared pan or mold. Refrigerate overnight.

TO SERVE: Unmold, remove paper, and slice with a knife that has been dipped in hot water. Make a puddle of melted jam on plate. Top with slice of pâte and garnish with fresh raspberries.

16 ounces quality bittersweet chocolate
3/4 cup red wine
1/4 cup heavy cream

seedless raspberry jam, melted
fresh raspberries (garnish)

Chocolate-Dipped Apricots

Go to this simple recipe when you need just a small taste of sweet . . . or want something to pass with coffee.

Melt chocolate in a small saucepan. Do not overheat; work on and off the heat. Stir until glossy. Dip half of each apricot into the chocolate. Place on piece of plastic wrap until chocolate sets. Store at room temperature.

semisweet chocolate chips
dried apricots

150

White Chocolate Grapes with Toasted Almonds

Very simple to do and breathtaking presentaton.

Wash grapes and place on rack over sheet pan.

Cut chocolate into pieces. Place in saucepan and gently heat on and off the heat. Do not overheat. Stir to remove all lumps. Drizzle over grapes. Sprinkle with toasted almonds. Refrigerate. Let chocolate set before removing to serving platter.

3 pounds white grapes
8 ounces white chocolate

2¹/4 ounces sliced almonds, toasted

TEACHING NOTES

Red Wine-Poached Pears   SERVES 6

A light dessert that can be done days ahead.

In a large nonreactive pan, combine wine, sugar, vanilla, salt, and peppercorns.

Evenly peel pears using a downward stroke beginning at the stem. Place in wine mixture. Bring to a boil and cook for 4 to 5 minutes. Turn off heat and allow to cool in liquid. Store in liquid in refrigerator.

1 quart red wine
1¹/4 cups sugar
1 teaspoon vanilla
pinch of salt
10 peppercorns

6 slightly underripe pears with stems

151

TEACHING NOTES

The hardest part of this recipe is dicing the fruit. It is necessary to hand dice the fruit before processing in the food processor.

Spray your hands with vegetable oil spray before rolling.

Fruit Mysteries

MAKES 24 TO 30 PIECES

I found this recipe from a newspaper clipping in my Mother's recipe box. I didn't remember it, but once I tried it, I was hooked . . . even with the vanilla pudding! It is a holiday staple.

In a large bowl, combine dates, apricots, and raisins. In food processor fitted with a steel blade, process fruit mixture. Add Chex and continue to process. Remove to large mixing bowl. Add pecans and coconut. Toss to combine.

Combine instant pudding powder, corn syrup, and lemon juice. Stir until well blended. Pour over fruit mixture. Mix lightly. Shape into 1-inch balls. Roll in shredded coconut.

To present, mound in a compote and sprinkle heavily with more coconut.

3/4 cup pitted dates, diced into tiny pieces

3/4 cup dried apricots, diced into tiny pieces

3/4 cup raisins

3 cups rice Chex

3/4 cup pecans, chopped

1 (3 1/2-ounce) can shredded coconut

1 (3 3/4-ounce) package vanilla instant pudding powder

1/2 cup corn syrup

2 tablespoons lemon juice

1 (3 1/2-ounce) can shredded coconut

French Meringues

MAKES 48 2-INCH MERINGUES

This method for making meringues can even be done on a rainy day!

Preheat the oven to 200 degrees. Place the egg whites in a large mixing bowl with a pinch of salt and 1 tablespoon granulated sugar. With an electric mixer, start at medium speed and beat for 2 to 3 minutes or until meringues are stiff. Increase the speed to high and add 1 tablespoon more sugar. When the egg whites are very stiff, add the remaining $1/2$ cup granulated sugar and beat for 30 seconds longer. By hand, gently fold the powdered sugar into the egg whites

Using a pastry bag fitted with #6 closed star tip, pipe the meringue onto parchment-lined (or grease and heavily flour pans) baking sheets. Place in preheated oven and bake for 2 to $2^1/2$ hours, being careful not to let them brown. Remove from oven and let cool. Store in airtight tin.

4 egg whites

pinch of salt

2 tablespoons plus $1/2$ cup granulated sugar

$3/4$ cup powdered sugar

DESSERTS

TEACHING NOTES

- *Egg whites should be at room temperature for greater volume. Forget to get them out of the refrigerator? Just place them in a bowl of warm water for 5 to 10 minutes. Bowls and utensils used for beating egg whites must be impeccably clean and grease free. And finally, there should be no traces of yolk in the whites.*

- *The flat roux whisk is perfect for folding egg whites. It goes more quickly and egg whites are not deflated.*

153

Mary James dishes it out

*To order additional copies,
visit www.maryjames.net or
Roosters Gourmet Market and Gifts
2417 C Lawndale Drive
Greensboro, North Carolina 27408*

*For more information, call
336-545-5785*